African American History

Slavery, The Underground Railroad, People Including Harriet Tubman, Martin Luther King, Jr., Malcolm X, Frederick Douglass and Rosa Parks [2nd Edition]

Copyright 2016 by Adam Brown - All rights reserved.

This document is geared towards providing exact and reliable information in regards to the topic and issue covered. The publication is sold with the idea that the publisher is not required to render accounting, officially permitted, or otherwise, qualified services. If advice is necessary, legal or professional, a practiced individual in the profession should be ordered.

- From a Declaration of Principles which was accepted and approved equally by a Committee of the American Bar Association and a Committee of Publishers and Associations.

In no way is it legal to reproduce, duplicate, or transmit any part of this document in either electronic means or in printed format. Recording of this publication is strictly prohibited and any storage of this document is not allowed unless with written permission from the publisher. All rights reserved.

The information provided herein is stated to be truthful and consistent, in that any liability, in terms of inattention or otherwise, by any usage or abuse of any policies, processes, or directions contained within is the solitary and utter responsibility of the recipient reader. Under no circumstances will any legal responsibility or blame be held against the publisher for any reparation, damages, or monetary loss due to the information herein, either directly or indirectly.

Respective authors own all copyrights not held by the publisher. Adam Brown is referred to as the author for all legal purposes but he may not have necessarily edited/written every single part of this book.

The information herein is offered for informational purposes solely, and is universal as so. The presentation of the information is without contract or any type of guarantee assurance.

The trademarks that are used are without any consent, and the publication of the trademark is without permission or backing by the trademark owner. All trademarks and brands within this book are for clarifying purposes only and are the owned by the owners themselves, not affiliated with this document.

ISBN 978-1-9992202-6-6 (Paperback)
Published by Pluto King Publishing

Table of Contents

Introduction   **10**

Chapter 1: The Beginning in Africa and the Slave Trade   **12**

Egypt   *13*
Ghana   *14*
Nigeria   *15*
Mali   *15*
Songhay Kingdom   *16*
Great achievements in science and technology in pre-slavery Africa   *20*
Math   *21*
Architecture and engineering   *22*
Medicine   *23*
Navigation   *24*
Maritime technology   *25*
Commerce   *25*
The slave trade era   *28*
The impact of the slave trade on Africa   *32*

Chapter 2: African Americans in the American Revolutionary War   **39**

Cato Howe   *41*
Colonel Louis Cook   *44*
Jack Sisson   *45*
Barzillai Lew   *45*
William Flora   *46*
James Armistead   *46*
Oliver Cromwell   *47*
Pompey Blackman   *47*
The Loyalists   *48*
Colonel Tye   *48*

Thomas Peters	49
Seymour Burr	49
Boston King	49
Henry Washington	50

Chapter 3: The Plantation Era — 52

Economic structure of the plantation era	52
Impact of economic growth on the social structure	53
Adverse economic effects of the plantation era	53

Chapter 4: The Biography of Harriet Tubman — 56

Escape from slavery	59
The American Civil War	60
Nicknamed Moses	61

Chapter 5: The Biography of Frederick Douglass — 66

From slavery to freedom	68
Women's rights	72
The Civil War and Reconstruction	72

Chapter 6: The Civil War and the Role of African Americans — 75

In the Union Navy	76
In the Union Army	76
Andrew Cailloux	78
Robert Smalls	79
William Jackson	79
William Carney	80
Aaron Anderson	80
Powhatan Beaty	81
Alexander Thomas Augusta	82
Miles James	82

    James Daniel Gardner   83
    John Lawson   83

Chapter 7: Jim Crow Laws   85
    Practical examples of Jim Crow laws   90
    Attempts at breaking the law   91
    The Great Migration   93

Chapter 8: The Great Migrations of African Americans   95
    The First Great Migration   96

Chapter 9: African Americans in World War I   99
    Henry Johnson   104
    Freddie Stowers   105

Chapter 10: African Americans in World War II   107
    Double V Campaign   108

Chapter 11: The Second Great Migration of African Americans   112
    Migration statistics   117

Chapter 12: The Civil Rights Movement   119
    What led to the civil rights movement?   121
    Martin Luther King, Jr.   124
    The Montgomery bus boycott, 1955   125
    March on Washington, 1963   127
    Malcolm X   128
    Rosa Parks   131
    The boycott   134
    South Carolina and Charleston's place in the civil rights movement   136
    South Carolina   139

Chapter 13: Dred Scott vs. Sandford — 143
How did this start? — 144
Economic consequences — 147
Political consequences — 147

Chapter 14: Black Feminism — 151
The post-slavery period — 153

Chapter 15: Black Lives Matter — 158
The impact of the Internet and social media on the movement — 160
BLM guiding principles — 161
Depictions in the media — 164

Conclusion — 166

Preview of "History of China" by Adam Brown — 167

Chapter 1: Ancient Chinese Dynasties — 167
Overview of Dynasties — 167
  1: Xia Dynasty (2200 – 1600 BC) — 167
  2: Shang Dynasty (1600 – 1046 BC) — 168
  3: The Zhou Dynasty (1046 – 256 BC) — 169
  4: The Qin Dynasty (221 – 207 BC) — 171
  5: The Han Dynasty (206 BC – 220 AD) — 172
  6: The Six Dynasties (220 AD – 589 AD) — 173
  7: The Sui Dynasty (581 – 618 AD) — 174
  8: The Tang Dynasty (618 – 907 AD) — 175
  9: The Five Dynasties (907 – 960 AD) — 177
  10: The Song Dynasty (960 – 1297 AD) — 178
  11: The Yuan Dynasty (1271 – 1368 AD) — 178
  12: The Ming Dynasty (1368 -1644 AD) — 179
  13: The Qing Dynasty (1644 – 1912) — 180

Chapter 2: Communism, Capitalism and Its Role in Shaping China & East Asia — **181**

China — *181*

East Asia, Asia, and the Pacific — *188*

Indonesia — *190*

Indochina — *190*

India — *191*

Introduction

Slavery is not the origin of Africa's history, as speculated and propagated by people ignorant of the rich history of the "Dark Continent." The opinion of such people is expressed in the words of David Hume, who said, "I am apt to suspect the Negroes to be naturally inferior to the Whites. There scarcely ever was a civilized nation of that complexion, nor even any individual, eminent either in action or in speculation. No ingenious manufacturer among them, no arts, no sciences." In the same vein, Gegel, a German philosopher in the 19th century, shared Hume's sentiment when he declared that Africa was not a part of the world.

Despite the emphasis placed on the enslavement of African Americans some centuries ago, slavery was a passing phase in history and never the defining stage of any single continent. While some people have ignorantly peddled incorrect information about slavery in North America, others have gone out of their way to combat the false views. The latter group has exposed the inaccurate information mentioned about African Americans as blatant lies and propaganda. They have done much to tell the other side of the story, replacing the lies with the real identity and history of African Americans. Fortunately, the truth is gaining momentum and gives African Americans at least some hope.

The goal of this book is to enlighten the reader about the rich history of African Americans. So many significant figures with grand achievements cannot go without mention. Some of their work was so influential that it continues today. Other important changes initiated by African Americans have become law as part of the United States Constitution.

You can look forward to reading the real story about:

- The role of African Americans in the Revolutionary War.

- The role of African Americans in World Wars I and II.

- Achievements of African Americans in the pre-slavery era.

- African American movements and the roles they played in the emancipation of African Americans both during and after the slavery era.

If you are interested in increasing your knowledge about African Americans in the past and the role Africa has played in world development, continue to the first chapter and read on. The first chapter will discuss Africa before the era of slavery. That will deepen your appreciation for the continent and its people. I do hope you enjoy this book and are able to share with others what you learn.

Chapter 1: The Beginning in Africa and the Slave Trade

African history is very broad and goes beyond the slave trade that ravaged the continent some centuries ago. It is an intricate subject that has been slightly altered by world-shaking events. From the pre-historic people who left their mark to those who initiated the slave trade, the image of Africa has meant different things to different people. While some people believe Africa has nothing to offer the world, others believe that Africa has contributed immensely to the development of the world at large. In spite of these conflicting opinions, Africa has held its ground in the face of undeserved criticism. It has continued to be the reference point in many areas of human endeavor.

The Trans-Atlantic Slave Trade that occurred between the 15th and 19th centuries had a dramatic negative impact on the economy of the continent. It also gave rise to distorted, biased views regarding the history of Africa. However, researchers have recently begun redressing the negative opinions about the continent and giving it its rightful place in world history.

The awesome contribution of the continent to world development is well documented. History has shown that the continent existed and enjoyed a huge measure of civilization before the arrival of the western slave masters. That is the absolute fact that has been covered by propaganda and misinformation.

It is imperative, then, to consider what history says about Africa before the era of transatlantic slavery, which took away many of its inhabitants to live in other lands. History has proven that Africa was never inferior to Europe, as its people had been living independently of Europe before the arrival of westerners. It is important to note that slavery was not a foreign concept; people of different tribes bought and sold slaves as a regular practice. Whenever one tribe fought another, prisoners would be left at the end. Those prisoners would often be sold as slaves. However, this slavery was not the same as that introduced by the Europeans and Americans. Those who were enslaved as a result of tribal conflict had rights, and their children did not necessarily become slaves; they were often born free. On the other hand, the slavery introduced by westerners was called chattel slavery. The children and grandchildren of slaves automatically became slaves themselves, and they did not have any rights. European slave traders slowed the pace of the continent's development when they offered to buy or take the slaves from those tribes that had slaves in Africa.

Right before colonization, Africa was a force to be reckoned with in some important sectors of the world economy. Before they were colonized, Africans excelled at science, technology, commerce, and other areas of human endeavor. The following is a consideration of the pre-slave-era achievements of some African countries.

Egypt

Some centuries before the continent was colonized, Egypt was a superpower in the areas of mathematics, science, technology and medicine. For thousands of years, the country set the pace in those fields, with no country strong enough to challenge its prowess. Egypt's magnificent achievements in those fields remain a reference point in history.

Before Rome came into existence and became a world power with its political and financial achievements, Egypt had enjoyed over 2,000 years of civilization. It is recorded that Egypt was the first world power to exist in history. This puts the African country far ahead of the Roman Empire, or any other world power, in terms of civilization.

Of course, two of the Seven Wonders of the Ancient World were found in Egypt, namely, the Great Pyramid of Giza and the Lighthouse of Alexandria. These were architectural masterpieces that were designed and built by Egyptians through personal efforts and a manual labor force before the invention of any machine. You cannot help but recognize the ingenuity behind the erection of those structures in the absence of cranes, cement mixers, block-making machines and other technologies that were developed later. In the field of medicine, too, Egypt was the clear leader before other countries could boast any serious achievements. The famous Pythagorean theorem was inspired by events that took place in Egypt, perhaps in relation to the pyramids.

The revered mathematician, Aristotle, acknowledged the role Egypt played in the field of mathematics when he wrote that "Egypt was the cradle of mathematics." This public acknowledgment is a proof of the advancement of Egypt and the indirect role the country played in advancing mathematics. Their contributions in the field of algebra and geometry, philosophy, architecture, mechanics and architecture contributed in a huge way to the development of the world today.

Egypt is not alone in this regard. There are many other African countries that had already established formidable civilizations before the arrival of westerners.

Ghana

Ghana is located in the region referred to as West Africa. Before the invasion of Africa, Ghana was a powerful force in the commercial sector. Due to the size of Western Europe, it was the business center of Africa between 800 and 1200 CE. Ghana's reputation as a commercial center was one of the reasons why foreign investors found their way to Africa.

Ghana's commercial activities included trading in natural resources such as salt, gold, and copper. The country was not formerly known as the Gold Coast for no reason; it was due to the abundance of gold in this country. Gold was the reason why Ghana was one of the most popular countries in Africa. In the pre-slavery era, merchants came from far and near to buy gold in Ghana. The country was so prosperous and advanced that the Ghanaian ruler during that era purportedly had a large army of more than 200,000 valiant men to protect his vast, rich empire. That was the extent of the power and achievement of Ghana even while many present civilized countries have no idea what civilization means.

Nigeria

Not to be left out are the Yoruba people in the southwestern part of Nigeria. They rocked the 11th and 12th centuries with their amazing sculpture and artwork. They led Ile-Ife and the Benin Kingdom with an unprecedented civilization in 500BC. The Yoruba people could be found in many African countries, including a large concentration in Nigeria. They were known for their handwork in wood, brass, ivory, and copper. Additional areas in which they excelled were pottery, ivory carving, gum and rope production, and other handiworks in which they could put their skills to use. Today, the artifacts made by the Yoruba people are still recognized and appreciated around the world for their quality and originality. On several occasions, people came from different parts of the world to purchase these artifacts due to their high quality.

Mali

Mali is one of the many African countries that held its own before the slave traders invaded the continent. This small African country was already a powerhouse before the slave traders came in the 15th century. The 13th to 15th centuries saw the achievements of the Mali Kingdom in the western and northeastern part of Africa. At the peak of the country's achievement in the commercial sector, agricultural produce and gold dust were produced in great quantities over the 2000 kilometers where the country carried out its organized trading. The country reached its commercial peak in the 14th century, some years before white men visited the continent with their slavery idea.

Songhay Kingdom

Between the mid-13th and mid-14th centuries, the Songhay Kingdom had its fair share of power and prosperity. Stretching from Mali to Sudan, the region practiced a well-organized system of government despite the absence of any European influence on the people and the government. The country gradually built a reputation as one of the best commercial places in the world. Universities and libraries were built and became the points of rendezvous for scholars, poets, and artists from the Middle East and other parts of the continent. Both in the academic and commercial sectors, the Songhay Kingdom was a success in Africa.

One of the biggest achievements of the kingdom was the well-known Islamic University of Sankore, also known as Sankore Madrasah or Sankore Masjid, located in Timbuktu. The university was established in the 14th century and the works of great philosophers were studied there. Some works of the Greek philosopher Aristotle and some branches of philosophy, grammar, law, astronomy, and the like were studied at the university. The country had almost a century of quality education in one of the best universities in the world where the working staff were scholars of African descent. Without foreign tutors, the University of Sankore built an enviable reputation as one of the greatest universities of its time.

According to Wikipedia, "By the end of Mansa Musa's reign (early 14th century CE), the Sankoré Masjid had been converted into a fully staffed Madrassa (Islamic school or in this case university) with the largest collections of books in Africa since the Library of Alexandria. The level of learning at Timbuktu's Sankoré University was superior to that of many other Islamic centers in the world. The Sankoré Masjid was capable of housing 25,000 students and had one of the largest libraries in the world with between 400,000 to 700,000 manuscripts."

History shows that Ahmed Baba, one of the most famous scholars of the school, wrote more than 40 books covering different areas of study, such as history, astronomy, and theology. His personal library was said to hold more than 1,500 volumes. Ahmed Baba is regarded in many quarters as the greatest scholar of that school. Ahmed Baba had no external influence to support his choice of career and contribution to his country. Yet, he carved an enduring niche for himself as a scholar of excellence in spite of his being an African without any European influence.

Not to be left out of this discussion is religion. Before whites came, Africa was deeply involved in various forms of religion. Africans practiced their religion passionately and achieved a measure of success with it. Prior to their claimed civilization, Christianity was practiced in Ethiopia before the Church of England was established there. The same can be said of Islam. Before Islam was extended to other parts of the world, Africans were practicing it, especially in the northern part of the continent. To convince yourself of these facts, just visit Rimbuktu. The Islamic city, as well as others like it, had universities and libraries where students studied astrology and advance mathematics years before Africa had a taste of foreign influence from slave traders.

Jewish, Islamic, and Biblical history is never complete without the mention of Africa. The Bible contains several references to African countries such as Egypt and Ethiopia, recognizing the existence of these countries even before the existence of the modern world. Yet, some are of the opinion that Africa wouldn't have survived without western influence. They believe that colonization brought religion to the continent. What an irony!

Some Greek scholars were regarded as the best the world has ever seen. The likes of Pythagoras, Hippocrates, Plato, Socrates, and the rest were revered as the best by their contemporaries. They are still held in high esteem today. Yet, these respected scholars were trained in Egypt, an African country. They were taught by Egyptian scholars who were not European but black people.

In an article titled "African Influence on Early Greeks," Josh Clark wrote: "It's well-documented that classical Greek thinkers traveled to what we now call Egypt to expand their knowledge. When the Greek scholars Thales, Hippocrates, Pythagoras, Socrates, Plato, and others traveled to Kemet, they studied at the temple-universities Waset and Ipet Isut. Here, the Greeks were inducted into a wide curriculum that encompassed both the esoteric as well as the practical."

The achievements of Ancient Egypt or Kemet still amaze us. These African people have the earliest record of civilization, which existed around the Nile Valley more than 5,000 years ago. Before Kemet rose to recognition, there seemed to be another kingdom called Ta Seti. That kingdom seemed to be in existence in Nubia, in today's Sudan. The kingdom was perhaps the earliest state recognized anywhere in the world.

Sadly, some modern historians have failed to give honor to those to whom honor is due. These historians regard the entire continent as having contributed nothing to global development. The civilization they propagate at the expense of the true value of Africans was nonexistent during the time of Mansa Musa. This African king singularly controlled all the gold value that could be found around the Mediterranean without resistance from any part of the world. He went down in history as the richest man who ever lived. This was in spite of the fact that he never used European technology to drive his business. He didn't have the Internet to help him. There was nothing like industrialization and yet he amassed his wealth the African way. This was a great achievement of which modern investors and inventors can only dream.

Some other notable civilizations recorded in history emanated from the Nile Valley, one of the greatest valleys in the world. The contributions of Nubi and KMT are proof of the role Africa and Africans played in civilization. Sadly, anti-black people are trying their best to deny the contributions of these kingdoms that are strategically located in Africa.

In that case, it is not out of the question for Africa to be rightly credited for its contributions to the scientific achievements that were recorded in Egypt. The African country produced great mathematicians as well as contributions to the fields of engineering and architecture.

This is a demonstration of the fact that the political, scientific, and economic developments in those African countries were perhaps better than in any other part of the world.

Prior to the 15th century, the African continent followed its well-defined path of development. It did this without the input of any countries outside the continent. In the centuries before the 15th century, Axum, Kush, the Great Zimbabwe, and Mali flourished before the intervention of the Europeans.

During those periods, some African countries had a good commercial relationship with China, India, and other Asian countries before the Europeans disrupted those relationships. For some centuries, Portugal and Spain were occupied by another African country after conquering the Iberian Peninsula in the 18th century. The invasion revealed the knowledge of African countries to Europe.

Long before their visit to Africa, some great empires existed in Mali, Ghana, and Songhay. These empires were built completely with proceeds from gold. The gold later provided Europe with the resources to build its economy two centuries before its invasion of Africa in the 15th century. It was the amazing wealth of Africa, especially the gold found in West Africa, that motivated the European countries to make their first visit to Africa.

By the time Africa was exposed to the outside world, the continent had already achieved much success in different areas of endeavor. Each country had functional political, economic, and social systems that contributed to its success. They maximized the opportunities offered by these systems to build the continent to the enviable standard it maintained before it was bastardized by European slave traders. In most parts of the continent, centralized states were alien to the culture. Most African countries worked under a policy that offered little encouragement for the division of power and wealth. Such societies thrived on internal democracy controlled by councils of elders and other institutions that worked together for the peaceful existence of the people within a particular country. Their internal unity and peaceful co-existence were responsible for the development of the continent as they worked on the principle of collective responsibility. Citizens believed in pulling together resources for the advancement of their communities. The achievements of these countries are proof of the practicality of their systems.

Both the eastern African country of Ethiopia and the western African country of Mali were an exception to the general rule of existence in Africa.

Although Mali and Ethiopia deviated a bit from the system of government practiced by most African countries with the influence of the Orthodox church in Ethiopia and Islam in Mali and in most parts of North Africa, African societies knew what worked for them and used those techniques to develop their countries before European intervention. Sadly, Africa has not received the credit it deserves for its numerous achievements. Rather, many people want to associate Africa with slavery alone, without considering what it had already achieved before foreign ideas were brought to the continent.

The development of Africa during the pre-slavery era was not limited to commerce. The continent has achieved some measure of success in other areas of life, such as science and technology. Let's consider some achievements in science and technology in pre-slave-trade Africa

Great achievements in science and technology in pre-slavery Africa

Despite the impact of sharecropping, slavery, and Jim Crow laws, ancient Africans contributed significantly to the development of science and technology. The achievements were recorded some 40,000 years ago, when civilization was a mirage. Sadly, only a handful of people are aware of the great contribution of Africans to science and technology.

It is quite unfortunate that only the Romans, Greeks, and other non-African scientists and inventors are usually mentioned in the same breath whenever the discussion centers on science and technology. In reality, their celebrated achievements came thousands of years after similar achievements were made in Africa.

While Egypt has always been the focus of technological and scientific achievements in Africa, sub-Saharan Africa also had impressive and sophisticated inventions. Africa had a good number of skilled inventors, including Ivan Van Sertima, who was an associate professor at Rutgers University. While the world has "deadened" its nerves to the geniality of African genius, a look at some of these achievements in science and technology will expose the falsehood under which our achievements have been hidden.

Math

Although Africa has not been credited for this achievement, the mathematics concepts that are taught in high schools were developed in Africa. The first counting method had its origin in Africa as well. Over 35,000 years ago, scripted mathematics textbooks on the multiplication and division of fractions and geometry formulas for calculating the volume and area of shapes were developed in Egypt, too. The Egyptians were able to calculate angles and distances, as well as use algebraic equations and other mathematical equations to make accurate predictions of the Nile River. According to them, a circle was 360 degrees and pi was an estimated value of 3.16.

The Egyptians also had an accurate understanding of the principles behind the Pythagorean Theorem when the theorem had not even been developed. They were aware of the three sides of a right-angle triangle if the sides are of the ratio 3-4-5.

Around 8,000 years ago, some countries in the western part of Africa developed their counting system, too. For instance, Zaireans had a numeration system before the slave traders arrived. The Yoruba people of southern Nigeria had a counting system. Their counting system used 20 as the counting unit rather than 10, which is used in modern times. According to experts, this counting system required a high degree of abstract reasoning to master.

Architecture and engineering

Past African empires made names for themselves in the field of architecture. An architectural masterpiece that readily comes to mind is the pyramids of Egypt. The largest pyramid in Egypt covers about 13 acres of land and was built with more than two million stone blocks. One of the pyramids built at Saqqara is the oldest of that type of structure in the world. The Great Pyramid held the record for world's tallest structure for some 3,800 years.

In Sudan, one can find more than 220 pyramids – more than in Egypt. That makes the country the home of the largest number of pyramids in the world. However, they were not the only architectural masterpieces in the continent before whites visited. Others that will leave you speechless include the obelisks found in Egypt. Mozambique and Zimbabwe also had some architectural designs that will hold you spellbound. In the 12th century, these countries made the hubs of their cities with massive stone complexes. One of those cities could boast a 15,000-ton granite wall that was 250 meters long.

In those cities, huge compounds were made in the form of castles with a good number of rooms designed for specific purposes. The 13th century witnessed the impressive cities of the Mali Empire, where there were awesome mosques, palaces, and universities. Timbuktu is a typical example of the grandeur of the Malian empire. Nigeria has some amazing architectural masterpieces, too.

One of them is the Walls of Benin, which was regarded as one of the largest manmade structure in the world before the British nearly destroyed it in 1897. When commenting on the Walls in The New Scientist, Fred Pearce wrote that: "They extend for some 16,000 kilometers in all, in a mosaic of more than 500 interconnected settlement boundaries. They cover 6500 square kilometers and were all dug by the Edo people. In all, they are four times longer than the Great Wall of China and consumed a hundred times more material than the Great Pyramid of Cheops. They took an estimated 150 million hours of digging to construct, and are perhaps the largest single archaeological phenomenon on the planet."

Another structure in Nigeria is the Sungbo's Eredo. The defensive walls were built in the southwestern part of the nation by the Yoruba tribes. This description aptly describes that awesome structure: "The total length of the fortifications is more than 160 kilometres (99 mi). The fortifications consist of a ditch with unusually smooth walls and a bank in the inner side of ditch. The height difference between the bottom of the ditch and the upper rim of the bank on the inner side can reach 20 metres (66 ft). Works have been performed in laterite, a typical African soil consisting of clay and iron oxides. The ditch forms an uneven ring around the area of the ancient Ijebu Kingdom, an area approximately 40 kilometres (25 mi) wide in north-south, with the walls flanked by trees and other vegetation, turning the ditch into a green tunnel."

Medicine

Most of the treatments used extensively today for a wide variety of ailments and diseases existed in Africa thousands of years before orthodox medicine was introduced by the European slave traders. From Nigeria to Egypt, Ghana to South Africa, the continent made several advancements in the field of medicine through the use of herbs and leaves for curing ailments. The herbs could cure pain and diarrhea, and some herbal extracts had efficient curative powers. Others were used for the treatment of malaria, cancer, and several other ailments.

Some of the medical discoveries of Africans include capsicum, ouabain, reserpine, and physostigmine. These local herbs were as effective as any orthodox medicine one can get today.

Some medical procedures carried out in Africa before Europe had any idea about them were autopsies, physiotherapy, vaccinations, limb traction, bullet removal, skin grafting, and anesthesia. These medical treatments were carried out under very hygienic conditions to prevent infections, thousands of years before they were introduced as the ideal condition under which medical treatments should be performed.

Navigation

Before the construction of huge vessels, Africans had built strong vessels they used for crossing the numerous waterways that dot the continent. Although Europeans are credited as the first people to make the voyage to the Americas, recent discoveries show that long before their voyage, Africans had visited some Asian and South American countries hundreds of years before the Europeans. All across Africa, boats, sailboats, and similar structures with the necessary facilities were built. Songhai and Mali were credited with building boats that were 13 feet wide and 100 feet long. Those boats could easily move 80 tons of weight on African rivers. The logic is very simple.

The currents from the Atlantic Ocean flow through some parts of West Africa on their way to South America. Ancient Africans plied that route on their way to the Americas because they found it convenient to do so. The 13th century also witnessed the sailing of Africans to China on different business trips. History has it that their cargo was elephants. Without automobiles, aircrafts, big ocean liners, and what have you, Africa made its way into other parts of the world centuries before the first automobile was introduced to the continent.

Maritime technology

In 1987, Fulani herdsmen from Nigeria discovered the oldest canoe in Nigeria near Dufuna village and the Yobe River. The boat was estimated to be 8,000 years old, making it the third oldest in the world. African mahogany was used to make the canoe. King Abubakar II, who ruled the Mali Empire in the 14th century, was said to have had ships on the coast of the western part of Africa. This story was attested to by Ibn Battuta, who recalled seeing hundreds of those ships. The major means of communication between these ships was drums. As a result, it has been speculated that Malian sailors may have reached America some 200 years before Christopher Columbus.

Commerce

African countries conducted their commercial activities with different items and metal objects. Some notable ones were gold, salt, copper, cowry shells, ingots, and other items. Cowries were used extensively as a medium of exchange in many parts of the continent as far back as the 11th century. They were used as legal tender in the western part of the continent until the 19th century. African countries carried out both internal and international trades with other countries with their medium of exchange before modern-day currencies were introduced.

So, with all these achievements before the invasion of the country by the Europeans, it would be unfair and a slap in the face of Africa and Africans to claim that Europe was responsible for all Africa's achievements. It is equally out of place to ascribe the achievements of Africa to other countries. Africa deserves her place among the developers of the world, regardless of what history says about it.

Hypocritically, nobody has ever come forward to deny the contributions of Greece to European civilization. Nor have they denied Ancient China its place and contribution to Asian civilization. The role played by Africa in the area of civilization was swept under the carpet. It is, therefore, a double standard and a show of hypocrisy to claim that Africa has never been part of civilization. It is part of the effort of some people to throw Africa into the dustbin of history. While that propaganda has been successful for years, its success won't last forever.

In his book *The Significance of African History*, the African-Caribbean writer Richard B. Moore rightly points out: "The significance of African history is shown…in the very efforts to deny anything of the name of history to Africa and the African peoples. For it is logical and apparent that no such undertaking [falsifying African history] would ever have been carried out and at such length, in order to obscure and bury what is actually of little or no significance."

What they have failed to realize is that the denial of Africa is the denial of history. The history of Christianity is African history. The same can be said about the history of Islam. One can't talk about the development of world civilization without mentioning the huge role Africa played in it. You simply cannot divorce Africa from the history of the world. Therefore, looking at the history of Africa from the perspective of slavery alone is a great injustice to the continent.

All these countries recorded their achievements before colonization and civilization. Why? The close-knit relationship upon which the continent was built was responsible for the pre-slave trade achievements of these African countries. Africans considered themselves to be one big family before slavery disrupted the continent. They did things together as brothers. That was the reason for their achievements.

In times past, Africans lived primarily on hunting and gathering. They lived in small communities with a few hundred people, and social bonds formed the basis of the love and unity among the people. Africans lived an interdependent life in which people hunted together and shared their food resources with love based on their communal unity. Africans moved away from their nomadic lifestyle around 14,000BC. That was a time when North Africa and the Sahara broke their dryness and became verdant. The green and fertile land encouraged farming and Africans in the area gradually used their newfound knowledge to the best advantage.

By 2500, the Bantu people had moved around Africa and later discovered the local iron-melting technology. They also used the new technology to develop new farming techniques that eventually put an end to the hunting and gathering lifestyle that was previously the only means of sustenance. This shows that the disparaging talk about Africa is uncalled for. Such people usually forget that China and Arabia were in a business partnership with Africa before the Europeans came. Before the Europeans arrived in China, Africans were already there, not in fetters, but as free business partners.

Africans knew about Europe before Europe claimed to discover Africa. What an irony! It defies any logic when people offer biased, hate-filled derogation of the continent, with remarks such as "pagan," "dark," "unorganized," and "licentious." It is for the benefit of such people that the history of Africa must be looked at from the right perspective, to eliminate any biases and inaccurate information about the continent. It was the invasion of whites that threatened the co-existence and achievements of Africans, not the other way around.

Issac Osei said that Africa had its own history before the Europeans found their way there. The Europeans were fascinated by what those who earlier came for business transactions saw. In the case of Ghana, the attraction was gold. The Europeans were so impressed that they came to Ghana to exchange some of their finished products in exchange for gold. Hence, they didn't come initially as slave traders, but as business partners. It was the introduction of slavery that changed people's perception of the continent. Africa was a thriving continent when Europeans first arrived.

The slave trade era

The slave trade was a turning point in the life and history of Africans. It remains the greatest tragedy that has befallen the world. In the history of humanity, nothing is a more significant social event than the African Holocaust that led millions of Africans into slavery to various parts of the world. The significance of the slave trade was not limited to the sheer number of victims; it also involves the horror and legacy attached to the Holocaust. The impact was huge. Humans with an enviable history and great culture were removed from history and reduced to mere commodities, traded in exchange for power and wealth. They were turned into insignificant labor units with a value less than the ground on which they walked.

An estimated 40 million to 100 million Africans were shipped to European countries as slaves via the Arabian, Atlantic, and Trans-Saharan routes. Millions of people also lost their lives in the struggle. Many died in transit, during slave raids, and while serving in foreign lands as slaves. Some millions more died of the trauma of leaving behind their homes, families, friends, and others for an unknown destination. Those people whose entire lives had been lived in the midst of their families and communities couldn't survive the ordeal. Others were victims of diseases during the long trip.

It is derogatory to call "slaves" those forcefully taken from their homes, farms, and workplaces. These were professionals who were separated from their sources of livelihood and forced to serve foreigners in foreign lands. Among them were mothers, fathers, and children. They were denied their freedom due to the selfish tendencies of some people.

When the Portuguese first visited Africa in the 1430s, they were interested only in gold. The country was synonymous with gold after the richest man in history, Mansa Musa, literally caused a depreciation of the value of gold on his route from Mali to Mecca. The king who was said to have a net worth of $400 billion gave gold as a gift on his way. He controlled half the total volume in the world. That gave him a massive net worth. His reputation drew the Portuguese to Africa to trade in gold. The first Portuguese traders were interested primarily in establishing a direct connection from Africa to Asia. When there was a growing need for domestic workers in most European countries and some sugar plantations in the Mediterranean, the Portuguese saw an opportunity to expand their business. They realized it would be more profitable for them to transport slaves from one location to another along Africa's Atlantic cost.

The Portuguese eventually started trading Africans for gold to merchants across Europe, to be used on plantations. By the 16th century, about 81,000 slaves had been shipped to various parts of the world as slaves. For over 2,000 years, Africans of different descent were forced into slavery. In just four centuries between 1500 and 1900, tens of millions of people from West Central Africa and West Africa were exported under the cruelest of conditions to serve as slaves. The blood and sweat of these black slaves served as the foundation of the enormous wealth and popularity enjoyed by the Americas and Europe till now.

When the New World was discovered, the European economy was given a huge boost. However, it had an equally negative impact on the African economy and history. From Brazil to the U.S., there was a huge need for laborers who could withstand the tropical climate needed for plantain plantations to thrive. An attempt to use the local Indians proved ineffective because the locals could not withstand the climate and broke down easily from the Old World-carried diseases. In addition, they were difficult to control. Hence, they saw in Africa a continent of strong and submissive laborers. They turned the continent into a continent of slaves.

In the 15th century, they found a permanent solution to the problem: slaves from Africa. The slave trade led to an influx of Africans to America, more than any other tribe because there was a huge demand for slavers in mining and on plantations. Most of these slaves were shipped to the Caribbean, Brazil, and the Spanish Empire. The leading slave traders were the Brazilians and Portuguese. The British came in third, while the Spanish and some other countries of the Cuban colony were also prominent slave traders. Other carriers were the Dutch, the West Indian Colony, and the French, as well as the Americans and the Danes.

Africans were later dispersed by European slave masters across the various countries of the Americas to serve under the most degrading and brutal conditions without a thought for their feelings and the people they had left behind. It is not strange, then, that millions of these slaves died in the process. Most of the surviving slaves were sold to other countries, where they worked on plantations in the Americas and the Caribbean – regions that were part of European civilization. They worked in plantations that produced tobacco and sugar to be shipped back to Europe for consumption.

The slave traders employed many effective strategies to get as many slaves as possible. Slaves were initially kidnapped along the Berber and Wolof villages on the coast of Northern Segambia. These slaves were made to work on the Iberian islands, where there was an avalanche of sugar cane and rice plantations. An increase in demand for laborers made the slave traders change their tactics. They turned to a more effective strategy: war. Because war had been the surest way to get slaves from time immemorial, they devised a means of generating warfare between nations.

Sometimes, they caused interracial war within a country to achieve their aim. From Angola to Senegal, one could hear drums of war across the continent. European companies, such as the British Royal African Company, the French Company of the West Indies, and the Dutch India Company, played most African rulers against each other. That resulted in a wave of wars throughout the continent. Realizing they could get more slaves from wars, the slave traders set greedy African leaders against each other. They turned them into middlemen with lots of attractive incentives to sell their citizens as slaves.

The Europeans did this by playing on those leaders' addiction to foreign items. Most of them were lured into it with a promise of firearms and alcohol. They were baited with these commodities and became willing tools in the hands of the slave traders. Eventually, the slave traders were able to get the best trade terms while the rulers enriched themselves from the proceeds of selling their brothers and sisters. Basic issues became civil wars, which gave the slave traders the opportunity to take sides with whomever they wanted. Those they supported were later used as the middlemen for their activities.

People were not free even during moments of peace. It was reported that farmers were not safe in their farms, as they could be kidnapped without warning by mercenaries who were usually royal slaves armed by the European slave traders. At night, villages were raided and men forced out of their homes. Houses were set on fire to increase tension among the people. The elderly were usually left to die while the strong were shackled and sent into slavery.

While those heated wars lasted, many prisoners of war were taken as slaves to foreign lands. That technique was very effective at finding more slaves for the slave traders while the continent lost some of its most able-bodied men. The loss of strong men to slavery reduced the continent to nothing. The continent eventually lost its power and was trampled upon by the slave drivers. That was the best technique until the Europeans came up with a more ruthless but less violent technique.

When the Europeans later realized the cost of sponsoring a series of wars and battles across the continent, they devised another strategy. They turned Africans against themselves. Brothers were set against each other. Rulers were bribed into selling their kinsmen. From one part of the continent to the other, the story was the same. Africans started selling their brothers into slavery in exchange for gifts. It was the most effective technique and had the greatest impact on the success of the slave trade and the decimation of the continent.

The impact of the slave trade on Africa

The trans-Atlantic slave business had a serious negative impact on the social, political, and economic aspects of Africa. A good look at the slave trade will reveal the degree of damage it did to the continent. Let's consider a few of these negative effects:

Famine: The cumulative effect of plundering, permanent warfare, and natural disaster plunged the continent into chaos. The once-prosperous continent had to struggle with epidemics and famine. Becuase most of the able-bodied men who could till the ground, farm, and provide for their families were either in slavery or dead in the wars, there were insufficient hands for agricultural purposes. The few fragile and hungry men left behind were dependents who were either sick or too old to work on the farm. The children had no farming experience and could do nothing to salvage the situation. As many more lives were also lost to diseases, famine was inevitable.

The economy of Africa went south. Africa could not provide enough for itself and was forced to make do with the little left behind by those taken into slavery. That led to an unprecedented level of hunger. The intensity of hunger and the hopelessness that swept through the continent forced some people to voluntarily offer themselves for slavery just to have a regular source of food. The continent was plunged into famine. From north to the south, east to west, famine ravaged the continent like a hurricane. The situation was pathetic.

Ethnic fragmentation: Ethnic fragmentation was one of the first negative impacts of slavery on the continent. It was not unusual for Africans to hunt and raid fellow Africans to capture and sell to European slave traders in exchange for commodities. There were heavy inter-village raids as well. Villages that had co-existed peacefully for centuries were turned against each other by slave traders, driving a wedge between them and putting a sudden and unexpected stop to their brotherhood. The bond between African brothers was broken and replaced by distrust and hatred.

The hostility generated by the slave drive led to inter-communal strife and wars. Communities rose up against each other and states bore arms to protect their members from being raided and sold into slavery. All the codes of conduct previously used to curb internal crises were thrown into the dustbin, with the protection for community members transcending any alliance or brotherhood. The situation degenerated drastically until more wars and clashes were necessary for protection against brothers who had suddenly become foes. African brothers became divided against each other overnight.

Social interaction also suffered. Communication between communities plummetted. Social groups that had served as a meeting ground for age groups from different communities became hostile. This was because of the degree of insecurity and the lack of trust occasioned by the suspicion of attacks. The rising incidences of banditry, conflicts, and suspicion due to the transatlantic slave trade led to an unprecedented degree of disintegration among African brothers. The seed of distrust produced a fruit that had a negative impact on the unity and spirit of brotherhood that was hitherto the underlying principle behind the peaceful coexistence of Africans.

Fragmentation of African states: The pre-slavery African states coexisted because peace and unity reigned supreme. They were their brothers' keepers and were always on the lookout for what would be mutually beneficial. All that became a part of history when the security of each state was weakened. There was a need for protection from invading slave traders. As each state made frantic efforts to protect its citizens, they needed weapons such as swords, knives, spears, firearms, and the like.

Ironically, these could be obtained only from the European slave traders. This was a problem that further increased the degree of hatred among Africans. The only way they could get those weapons was in exchange for slaves. This meant states had to prey on the citizens of other states to get slaves they could sell in exchange for weapons. As the need for protection increased, there was also a corresponding increase in the need for slaves. That obviously meant there was an increasing need for the security of neighboring states to be breached at will and the citizens forcefully taken and sold into slavery. That created a huge tension among sovereign states.

The peace they both enjoyed became a forgotten history. More weapons were needed. More slaves had to be captured in exchange for weapons. And the more that each state met its goals, the more the continent disintegrated as a result of sovereign states enslaving one another for their own selfish gains: protection and security. Intracontinental strife took over the landscape as more countries were out to protect their citizens. That fragmented the continent further.

A typical example of the extremes to which some countries went to ensure security and protection for their members was the incident that occurred in the Kabre community, a prosperous community in Togo, in the 19th century. This community reportedly captured its members and sold them into slavery for an opportunity to get more ammunition to beef up their defense against external invasions. So, while fighting external aggressors, they engaged in the same act from which they were protecting their members. They prevented slave traders from invading their community but voluntarily sold the locals into slavery. What an irony!

Political implications: Aside from the economic impact, the slave trade had a serious political impact on the populace. Political relationships were strained and friendships faced trust issues. The story was never the same, as people found it difficult to trust each other in the face of the degree of betrayals they had witnessed from their kings. The tyranny and brutality of the attacks remained indelibly written in the hearts of many people. Africans lost nearly everything to slavery; the geographical entity known as Africa has never been the same. Political upheaval, civil unrest, and other challenges emanating from the slave trade have not subsided. They left a deep wound in the political heart of Africans that has refused to heal over time. According to Curtin, the political instability the African states experienced was a result of European intervention in the continent while they searched for slaves. Because most of the participants in the trade were rewarded and received many slaves for their efforts, the Europeans went so far as to intervene in political processes. They thereby created conflicts and internal instability to achieve their goals.

Due to the handsome rewards for participants in the slave trade, people did anything to sell their kinsmen. This included community leaders. Either by coercion or voluntarily, they sold their people in exchange for knives, clubs, or whatever the Europeans offered them. For instance, the involvement of chiefs and other political leaders in the trade led to an expected loss of trust in the political system. The existing system gradually lost its grip on people as each individual or family head took the security of their family members into their own hands. Gradually, the political system, especially the community leaders, became a mere puppet in the hands of the slave traders and lost any iota of trust the people had in them.

A typical example of such an aberration occurred in the Kongo Kingdom. This was a powerful kingdom in West Central Africa before the first European stepped on African soil. In 1514, local Kongo citizens were kidnapped by their leaders and sold to European slave merchants from Portugal. The slave trade became so rampant, it created unprecedented political and social disorder in the kingdom. Over time, the kingdom collapsed as the king lost his authority completely. That was a typical example of the impact of the slave trade on the political landscape of Africa. Many other political institutions faced a similar fate at the hands of their subjects. It was a big blow to the continent.

The legal system: The slave trade hit the legal system hard. Prior to slavery, the legal system was the last hope of the masses. The verdict of the members of the local court was final. However, things took another turn when the same legal system was used to force innocent citizens out of the continent and form slave labor in foreign lands. The legal system was bastardized by the slave traders who bought the local judiciary in exchange for exotic items.

Before their invasion, most African countries had created and trusted judicial systems with established punishments for various crimes. That made the legal system the go-to for the masses whenever there was a dispute or a violation of the law. The exploitation of the system was a huge blow to the masses. It denied them unrestrained access to justice. False accusations became the perfect means through which a citizen found himself on the next boat taking slaves away from the continent.

Slave merchants falsely accused their fellow Africans of every trumped-up charge one can imagine. People were accused of witchcraft, sedition, and other false accusations. Gradually, the established punishments for those offenses were altered to suit the white slave traders. With sudden and illegal constitutional amendments, the punishment for any crime was slavery. Former punishments such as beatings, excommunication from the village or community, exile, and compensation became obsolete. Slavery, as the new form of punishment, took center stage and reigned supreme. That created palpable fear among the people. People were no longer assured of their freedom, as someone could level a false accusation that would land someone else in slavery without a hearing. The abuse of the judicial system was pathetic.

Let's consider the case of a Cassanga chief in what is today Guinea Bissau. The chief committed a great atrocity in his effort to satisfy his personal desires by embarking on a gross abuse of the local judicial system. According to Hawthorne (1999, 2003), the Cassanga chief procured slaves for the slave merchants by using what is commonly called the red water ordeal. In this case, people accused of any crime were not subjected to the local laws and punishment. Rather, the chief forced those purported criminals to drink a poisonous liquid.

Those who vomited the poison were convicted of the crime and immediately sold into slavery. Their possessions were taken by the chief. Those who were not lucky enough to vomit later died of poisoning. The chief would also forfeit the poisoned native's possessions and sell the family members of that person into slavery. This blatant abuse of the system led to its death, as people lost their trust in a system that had become a willing tool of selfish slave merchants. The system that had been credible before the Europeans subsequently became the enemy of the people.

Communal displacement: Slavery also triggered unprecedented communal displacement throughout the continent. Many communities were displaced and had to seek temporary refuge in neighboring villages and communities. The slave traders' attitude towards the people necessitated that. After capturing slaves, these merchants transported them via many routes to the coast. These coasts were the meeting points of the merchants, and were where slaves were collected before being shipped to Europe.

It was customary for the slave merchants to collect slaves along their routes while heading towards the coast. As a protective measure against becoming a victim, most communities along those routes were forced to move due to their fear of being caught. It was the only measure to prevent becoming a victim of the circumstances. During this era, millions of Africans were displaced across the continent.

Displacement negatively affected the economy of the continent. While residents were in flight, many productive activities were left behind. Farming, which was the primary source of livelihood, was abandoned. Homes were abandoned. Other sources of livelihood were left behind while people ran for their lives. They couldn't afford to wait and lose their freedom. This also contributed to the famine that swept through the continent during that era. The economy of the continent suffered a downturn.

The slave trade touched every aspect of people's lives. They lost everything they once had in abundance. Homes were lost. Families were separated. Trust was broken between brothers. The legal system was compromised and bastardized. Famine hit the continent like a raging storm. Africa suffered immensely from slavery. The continent has never fully recuperated from the negative impact of slavery.

Chapter 2: African Americans in the American Revolutionary War

African Americans played a huge role in the American Revolutionary War. From the first shot that announced the beginning of the war to the ultimate victory at Yorktown, the role of African Americans cannot be ignored. Black men of African origin contributed significantly to the emancipation of the United States from Great Britain.

On March 5, 1770, the Boston Massacre fueled the embers of agitation for freedom. At the center of the agitation was an escaped slave, Crispus Attucks. One of the first of the many African Americans who gave their lives for the struggle was Prince Estabrook. On April 19, 1775, in Massachusetts, he paid the ultimate price for the quest for freedom. That same day, many African Americans put their lives on the line to offer maximum protection to the Concord Bridge without second-guessing their decision to do so.

When the Battle of Bunker and Breed's Hill was underway, more than a dozen African Americans took part. They fought gallantly for the independence of America, their skin color notwithstanding. One of the outstanding fighters in that battle was Cuff Whittenmore. He was recognized for his bravery and was permitted to take possession of a sword he had taken from a British officer for "fighting bravely." Many other African Americans followed in the footsteps of this valiant fighter and gave their all to the war.

Peter Salem was another black soldier with exceptional fighting skills. He was a member of the troop that took part in the Battle of Concord in April 1775. He also took part in the battle popularly known as the Battle of Bunker Hill. For killing a senior British officer in the Battle of Concord, 14 American officers including Colonel William Prescot and other members of the group to which Salem belonged were rewarded for their efforts in ensuring victory for America. It is interesting to note that this African American officer was the only soldier singled out for such praise among the approximately 4,000 soldiers in that unit. He was recognized for his outstanding bravery, and many people signed a document in honor of "a brave and gallant soldier." This petition was sent to the General Court of the Massachusetts Bay Colony for approval. The Court went on to say that the black soldier "behaved like an experienced officer." That was a deserved recognition for this brave fighter.

According to a document that profiled the activities of the unit, Salem Peter was originally sent to Bunker Hill with two other soldiers to build fortifications. Although the details of the exploits that earned him such praise are not known, the petition makes it clear that "to set forth the particulars of his conduct would be tedious." This is an indication that his heroic deeds were numerous and awesome. For a black fighter to be given such adulation, he must have done something exceptionally brilliant, something out of the ordinary.

When John Trumbull painted an image of the battle, he included two black soldiers in his portrayal of the battle scene. This was in recognition of the huge role black men played in the war. A similar recognition was given in *Washington Crossing the Delaware*, an 1851 painting by Emanuel Leutze. In his painting, the artist included a black soldier supporting Washington in the boat as they crossed the river to battle. The crossing and the valiant display of Salem and his colleagues eventually resulted in a victory for his side on December 26, 1776 at Trenton, New Jersey.

Other notable battles in which Salem took part were Stony Point and Saratoga. At Stony Point on July 16, 1779, he was a member of the Continental Army of George Washington, who had an upper hand in a battle against British troops. The battle was known for its promptness and swift victory. The heavy losses suffered by the British troops in that battle went down as one of the most important victories the American troops recorded in the war.

In the battles of Saratoga, which took place on September 19 and October 7, 1777, Peter Salem fought alongside his troop members in a battle that put an end to the Saragota campaign. The troops gained a victory over their British contemporaries. This was one of the decisive victories that gave the Americans much-needed foreign support to gain a complete victory over Britain. It was one of the earliest victories in a series that helped America win the Revolutionary War. In all these battles, this African American played a huge role in ensuring his regiment achieved its deserved victory over the opposing army.

Cato Howe

Cato Howe played an important role in the Revolution, too. This courageous African American served as a member of the American troops as a spy. As a member of the Black Patriots, his responsibility was to gather valuable information and intelligence for the American troops. It was a risky assignment that could cause his death if he were caught by the British troops. Yet, he gathered the necessary information, giving his side confidential information to win some battles.

According to a historian, Cato was one of the most intelligent fighters in his regiment. His intelligence was one of the attributes that contributed significantly to the success of his group. The contribution of these black soldiers was not limited to the Army. They also contributed to the war in many other ways.

For instance, African Americans served in the Navy to have the opportunity to participate fully in the war. Due to the hazards of fishing, the sea, and other potential challenges, the Navy was always in need of crewmen. As such, it had no restrictions on enlisting black people. Regardless of skin color, they enlisted people from different backgrounds. The only requirement was a willingness to serve. Many African Americans met that requirement and served wholeheartedly in the war.

The open door policy employed by the Navy encouraged many black men to join the struggle for the liberation of America from slavery. While the U.S. Marine Corps was in its infancy, black recruits were welcomed to offer needed support. More than a dozen of these African American fighters fought on the side of America on U.S. ships. Apart from their support of the United States, some black soldiers also supported American rebels. For instance, the French troop was made up of 3,500 fighters.

However, more than 600 of those fighters were black and on the side of France in their attempt to take over Savannah, Georgia, in 1779. They were black slaves and freemen recruited from some of the French Caribbean colonies. Bernardo de Galvez, a Spanish governor, also hired some black soldiers to support his campaign when fighting against the British in the Gulf Coast and the Mississippi Valley. Apart from the U.S., the greatest beneficiary of the availability of African Americans for the war was Britain. The British government capitalized on loopholes in U.S. government policies with respect to African Americans' inclusion in the military. Thus, Britain was able to enlist a good number of willing African fighters into its army.

Some slave traders did not support the enlistment of black soldiers, the majority of whom were slaves. The slave traders took this stand to protect themselves from losing some of their slaves to the war. Some Americans were also apprehensive about the possible consequences of arming a slave to fight. They were conscious of the possibility of an uprising that may eventually have a negative impact on their lives and businesses. It was in light of this that Massachusetts issued a resolution forbidding the inclusion of slaves in battle. According to the Massachusetts resolution, no slave would be permitted to join the Army regardless of the situation. On July 10, 1775, Washington sent another order forbidding the enlistment of African Americans in the Revolutionary war. The order read: "You are not to enlist any stroller, Negro, or vagabond."

Washington and his cronies did not tolerate black fighters in their armies. They didn't want to give black slaves opportunities to fight for their freedom, although they were helping America fight for its freedom from its colonial master, Britain. America's negative stand gave Britain an opportunity to increase the numerical strength of its army by opening its doors to these black soldiers. Escaped slaves were welcomed en masse by Britain to exploit American prejudice towards black fighters and beefed up their army without a second thought.

To further encourage slaves to enlist in the British army, the following proclamation was issued by John Murray, the royal governor of the colony of Virginia and the Earl of Dunmore, on November 7, 1775: "I do hereby declare all indentured servants, Negroes or others free, that are able and willing to bear arms, they joining His Majesty's troops, as soon as you may be, for the more speedily reducing this Colony to proper dignity." What was the result of the proclamation?

The allure of freedom was so irresistible, many slaves risked everything to make a trip to Britain. In less than a month, more than 300 slaves were integrated into the "Ethiopian Regiment." These newly recruited soldiers were given all the paraphernalia of office, including uniforms that were emblazoned with an apt slogan: "Liberty to Slaves."

Eventually, more than 30,000 former slaves went on the promise of freedom offered by Dunmore. While the Ethiopian Regiment faced battle, some provided technical support and other support services, serving as cooks, wagon masters, and laborers. Some took up unusual jobs. For instance, Bill Richmond served as the executioner of a rebel spy, Nathan Hale, in 1775 in New York. By the end of the war, more than 20,000 black soldiers had pledged their allegiance to the British. They preferred an uncertain future with the British to a return to their old masters in America. Hence, many African Americans ended up in Britain, Canada, Europe, and the West Indies.

The mass exodus of slaves to Britain forced Washington to reconsider his exclusion policy. Washington issued a counterorder on December 10, 1775 that allowed free blacks to be considered for enlistment, though he still maintained his stand on slaves. Washington's subordinates took to this new instruction and recruited as many black fighters as they could, ignoring the ban on the enlistment of slaves. They considered the status of the black soldiers insignificant. They desperately needed to catch up with Britain and did everything they could to increase their army with black fighters.

This action drastically increased the number of black fighters who participated on both sides of the war. Both sides recruited African American fighters until the end of the war. Black women were not exempted from the war, either. Although they did not carry arms, they provided other forms of support. As part of their contribution to the war, black women served in different capacities. They were actively involved in the war by chronicling it. When the soldiers needed blankets and uniforms, black women sewed them.

During the war, the injured and wounded soldiers received proper assistance and care from these women. Black women worked around the clock to provide moral and medical support for the soldiers. The prompt medical care facilitated the recuperation of many wounded fighters and meant the Army didn't have to be without soldiers for long. During the Revolution, many black fighters stood out for their bravery and exploits. In addition to Mr. Peter mentioned above, other notable fighters of African origin are:

Colonel Louis Cook

Louis Cook was the commander-in-chief in charge of the Continental Army under George Washington. He fought gallantly against the British army. He was christened Colonel Louis by George Washington himself in recognition of his bravery and achievements. He carried out a series of attacks against the opposing British troops. On a number of occasions, he led the troops from the front. In March 1778 General Philip Schuyler gave him an order to ensure the complete destruction of all the British ships stationed at Niagara.

He was commissioned as a lieutenant colonel by the Continental Congress. Cook was the first and probably only soldier of African heritage to get promoted to that rank during the Revolution. This is a proof of his efficiency and contribution to his regiment.

Jack Sisson

Jack Sisson was one of the valiant soldiers who captured General Richard Prescot of the British army in July 1777. Sisson was among the 40 soldiers who risked their lives to breach the security provided by British-controlled waters. They sneaked up on the British general and captured him. Some accounts claimed that Sisson broke the general's door with his head before capturing him. During a mission, he even took charge of a boat. In all the missions in which Jack participated, no soldier was lost.

Barzillai Lew

Barzillai Lew was an African American soldier who displayed exceptional fighting skills during the Revolutionary War. He was called to join the Army, which he did on May 6, 1775, under Captain John Ford's 27th Regiment in Massachusetts. He was also one of the black fighters who showed impressive courage during the Battle of Bunker Hill, which took place on June 17, 1775. The military records describe him as being a quick and large man. He was a six-foot-tall fighting machine.

The Bunker Hill battle was one that both sides of the war would not forget. The American army lost 140 troops, while 301 were wounded and another 30 were captured in battle. The British forces did not fare better. They lost 226 troops and 828 were wounded. Lew established a good reputation in this battle. It is on record that he boosted the morale of the troops with his words of encouragement through his powder horn. The powder horn he used during the war is now one of the collections found in the DuSable Museum of African American History, located in Chicago, Illinois. It was donated to the museum by the war veteran's great-great-grandson, who is also the co-founder of the museum.

William Flora

There's a good reason why William Flora was hailed as a hero for his performance at the Battle of Great Bridge. He was a free black soldier who put all his efforts into fighting alongside American troops during the Revolutionary War. During one of his missions, he displayed heroic acts by ripping up the planks of a bridge to permanently halt the progress of the advancing Redcoats. He did that at the risk of his life, as he was under fire. After the war, he went on to set up a business from which he made a small fortune.

James Armistead

James Armistead was another African American whose contribution to the Revolution was recognized. This former slave to William Armistead served as a substitute for military service during the war. In 1781, he made his personal decision to spy on the invading British forces. He subsequently applied to the military and was accepted by the American General Marquis de Lafayette. While serving in the field, he proved his mettle and gained the confidence and trust of Lord Cornwallis, a British general.

He later sold valuable information he gathered from the British army to the American forces. That gave the Americans an edge over the British. Subsequently, during the Battle of Yorktown, which was one of the fiercest battles, the American forces got the upper hand over their British counterparts. Although many people consider Armistead to be the first double agent in the world, his contributions to America's victory cannot be ignored. He later petitioned the Virginia assembly in 1786 and was freed from slavery as a reward for his heroic efforts during the war.

Oliver Cromwell

Oliver Cromwell was in his 20s when the war broke out. He was born in Burlington County, New Jersey in 1753. Although he planned to become a farmer, he abandoned that and joined the military in support of the United States. With the Second New Jersey regiment, he was on the battlefield in Brandywine, Princeton, and Monmouth. During the 1776 river crossing on Christmas Day, he was among the troops who crossed the river successfully. George Washington personally signed his discharge papers after the war. When the war was over, Cromwell lived on a military pension for the rest of his life.

Pompey Blackman

Pompey Blackman was an African American private during the Revolutionary War. He was born in 1755 and played a crucial role during the war. Pompey was initially known as Pompey Blackman or Pompey Fortune before he was later identified as Pompey Freeman in 1785. He was born during the slave era, although his slave status remains unknown. He joined the Massachusetts regiment in April 1775 before switching to another regiment under Loammi Baldwin. He was an active African American fighter during the American Revolution.

Pompey fought in the Battles of Bunker Hill and Lexington. He was an active member of the colonial troop that prevented the British troops from exiting through Boston as part of an effort to reduce the British troop's ability to damage the American troops. After the evacuation of the British army from Boston, Pompey joined the regiment of General Benedict Arnold and fought the British army in New York. Under the 15th Massachusetts regiment, he served a total of three years before he was finally discharged in November 1780.

The heroes profiled above worked for the interest of America during the Revolutionary War. They gave their maximum support to the country and ensured its freedom from Britain.

However, some Africans pledged their allegiance to Britain during the war. Although they didn't win the war, they played some outstanding roles in it. Following are some of these loyalists.

The Loyalists

The promise of freedom made by Lord Dunmore, the governor of Virginia, to any slave who joined the British forces caused many African Americans to liaise with the British forces during the war. Dunmore promised to grant freedom from rebel masters to whoever joined them in what is generally known today as "Lord Dunmore's Proclamation." The result was unbelievable. Thousands of slaves who were previously serving under the most inhumane conditions on plantations made a drastic change and moved en masse to join the British army.

For the sake of history, these former slaves turned freedom fighters deserve a mention.

Colonel Tye

Tye's original name was Titus Cornelius. The African American slave served in the British army. His loyalty as a guerrilla leader and his tactical leadership ability and skills impressed the British army so much, he was given the honorary title of colonel. His first action on record as a military man was at the famous Battle of Monmouth in 1778, when he captured an America captain. In the following year, he fought many battles and took many prisoners. Many slaves received their freedom from him while he tormented the American Continental Army by seizing its fuel and food. He was so tactically skilled that the American forces had a real struggle before they could wrestle New York City away from the British forces.

Thomas Peters

The town of Freetown in Sierra Leone was founded by four people, including Thomas Peters. He was born into slavery and changed hands among slave masters and traders a couple times. When the war was underway, Peters escaped to North Carolina to join the British troops. He subsequently became a member of the Black Loyalist Regiment and was later promoted to the rank of sergeant. Twice, he felt the full impact of the war when he suffered serious wounds while fighting the American forces.

When the war was over, Peters and other freed slaves headed to Nova Scotia in Canada in the company of the British army. He then made his way to England to champion the cause of resettling African Americans back home in Sierra Leone. His trip to England was successful. Almost 3,500 people from the continent moved back to Africa with him. He died peacefully in Freetown in 1792.

Seymour Burr

Seymour Burr fought on the side of Britain during the Revolutionary War. Seymour was his only name until he escaped from slavery to join the British army after being convinced by Lord Dunmore's Proclamation to fight against the American Continental Army. However, his goal was to seek his freedom. When he attempted to run, he was captured and returned to his master. After receiving a favorable bargain from his master, he enlisted in the Continental Army and fought against the British troops.

Boston King

Boston King was a contemporary of Thomas Peter. He joined Peter and two other people as the founding fathers of Freetown, Sierra Leone. He was also born into slavery like Peter and grew up as a professional carpenter. He made decided to join the British army when he got wind of Lord

Dunmore's Proclamation. When the war was over, Boston and his wife were commissioned to move to Nova Scotia. From there, he migrated back to Africa, to Freetown.

He was a Methodist minister and later became Sierra Leone's first missionary. In his autobiography, he recounted his experiences during the war and resettlement.

Henry Washington

Henry Washington was a personal slave of George Washington, America's first president. He was responsible for maintaining the horses of this famous American leader at Mount Vernon. In 1776, he heard Lord Dunmore's Proclamation and took his chances, joining the popular Ethiopian regiment when the regiment was close to New York. Throughout the war, he pledged his unflinching loyalty to the African American Loyalist.

Washington moved to Nova Scotia with his family. From Nova Scotia, he moved to Africa before he eventually moved to Sierra Leone around 1791. His quest for freedom was far from over. When the locals rebelled against the mistreatment meted out to them by the Sierra Leone Company, Washington participated in the rebellion and ensured the restoration of freedom and equality among his African brothers.

The African Americans who were on the side of the British troops during the Revolutionary War had a reputation for strength and bravery. They used everything at their disposal to fight for a cause in which they believed. Although they were not immediately given the freedom and equality they deserved, they used the opportunity to let the world hear their voices.

Most black slaves looked to the British forces for hope. They expected Britain to assist them with their liberation. No wonder some of them decided to pledge their allegiance to the British troops. When one of the British generals, General Cornwallis, made his way into Carolina between 1780 and

1781, an army of black slaves went with him. When the British army sailed from Charleston in 1782, some 5,000 African Americans sailed with the troops. In the end, more than 3,000 African Americans left the shore of America from New York, with most of them heading towards Nova Scotia, Canada.

Whether they were fighters or worked as domestics serving either side, valiant African Americans played key roles in the Revolutionary War.

Chapter 3: The Plantation Era

The plantation era occurred at a significant time in American history, when the southern United States grew its economy based on plantation farming with the assistance of African slaves. That was between the late 1700's and the beginning of the American Civil War. The higher percentage of economic development recorded during that period was the result of the increasing value of the plantation farming system, with black slaves providing the labor force.

Of course, many historians considered the economic woes the South faced soon after slavery was abolished to be proof that the slave trade was the pillar of the plantation era. Prior to the Civil War, a sharp rise in the degree of large-scale farming in the South and plantation slavery was noticed. The story changed immediately after the end of the war. Therefore, it is important to study the economic importance of slavery to the South.

Economic structure of the plantation era

The South witnessed a sharp expansion in the agricultural sector during the plantation era, while the manufacturing sector that was the main source of income for the North experienced slow growth. One of the characteristics of the Southern economy during that period was capital accumulation at a very low level. The economy also experienced a sharp reduction in its liquid capital. When this was combined with a focus on staples and the decline of the Southern banking sector, the South eventually had to depend on export trade for survival.

Unlike the West and the North, which depended exclusively on what their domestic markets could generate, the South depended on the West for sustenance commodities while the North provided manufactured goods. During this period, the agricultural economy of the South was built on grain, sugar, cotton, rice, and tobacco. Other places such as Alabama,

Mississippi, and Louisiana – referred to as the Deep South – produced cotton and other cash crops. It was not surprising that the end of the war negatively affected the economy of the South. This was the result of losing a higher percentage of their labor force to the war. Many of their slaves joined the war and never returned, while some gained freedom after the war. That had a negative impact on their economy.

Impact of economic growth on the social structure

As more slaves were brought into the region, indentured servitude was effectively displaced, making slavery the major supply of labor for all Southern plantations. The economic implications of slavery as an institution facilitated the uneven spread of wealth in the slave-dependent South. Gradually, there was an increasing demand for more slaves to help in the plantations. Supported by the government's clampdown on importing more slaves into the country, there was a sharp increase in the value of slaves. This led to a corresponding increase in the prices of slaves, making small farmers benefit greatly from selling their slaves.

Those in the inner part of the South, like Virginia, could sell their slaves to the West or farther south for a profit. Because small farmers stood a great chance of losing their slaves to disability and death, these farmers couldn't risk that chance when they could still make money from selling their slaves. The rise in the prices of slaves led to the joint ownership most farmers practiced shortly before the outbreak of the Civil War.

Adverse economic effects of the plantation era

The plantation era was responsible for the economic growth of the South and also for the decline in the region's productivity from the early to middle 19th century. Due to the huge volume of labor the plantation system required, the South lacked the wherewithal to meet human resources requirements for success at the expiration of the plantation era. The problem was aptly described by Ulrich Bonnell Phillips when he contended that the system was favorable to some people "who would have been otherwise capable of performing other skilled jobs were nonetheless relegated to field work because of the nature of the system." The relegation of such skilled people to unskilled labor was definitely suicidal for the economy of the South.

As a result of its dependence on slave labor, the South wasn't prepared for the industrial boom. Hence, it was overwhelmed by the demand for skilled labor necessary to drive the economy. The South had no option other than to rely on the abundance of skilled hands in the North. Commercially, the South couldn't survive independently of the North.

The plantation era played a significant role in the lives of the Africans working as slave laborers in plantations. According to history, it was the great demand for more laborers in sugarcane and other plantations that triggered the use of slaves. As the need for slaves increased, more Africans were captured and forcibly sold into slavery.

Although slaves were usually assigned different jobs, most of them were assigned to work in plantations where many hands were required to handle the tedious jobs that running a plantation required. Sugar plantations were considered one of the most labor-intensive types of plantations, where slaves of different sexes and ages were required to put in a minimum of 12 hours of work a day. The skills expected of a slave depended on the type of plantation where he or she worked. Cultivating and processing sugar required a wide variety of skills which were quite different from the skills required on a tobacco or rice plantation.

To the relief of plantation owners, Africa was blessed with men skilled at different handiworks. Thus, they could easily find the skilled labor for work on a plantation. There were blacksmiths, carpenters, sugar boilers, coopers, and potters. These jobs were usually assigned to male slaves. It is on record that more men than women were exported to Europe as slaves. More plantation owners preferred men to women due to the degree of physical strength required to be useful on a plantation. However, some plantation farmers preferred female slaves to work on their plantations.

Slaves usually worked long hours on the plantation. Those working on plantations were the worst hit. These slaves usually started before dawn and were at work until after sunset. Sometimes, they could get two-hour breaks in the afternoon for lunch.

Of course, white farmers had a reputation for working long hours, too. However, the difference lay in the degree of freedom the farmer enjoyed. While the farmer had absolute control of his time, the slaves could not dream of such a luxury. Black slaves worked under strict supervision, to which the farmers were not subjected. The threat of any form of punishment was another challenge with which constantly dealt. This forced them to work under the worst conditions, as they feared the most inhumane punishment that could be meted out to them.

Chapter 4: The Biography of Harriet Tubman

Harriet Tubman was born around 1822 as Araminta Ross in Maryland. Her parents were slaves named Ben Ross and Harriet Green. Green was Mary Pattison Brodess' slave and was later transferred to Mary's son, Edward. Ben was the property of Anthony Thompson (the owner of a large plantation near the well-known Blackwater River in Maryland), whom Mary wed.

Ben Ross was a skilled carpenter and in charge of the timer work on his master's plantation. Harriet Green was the Brodess family's cook. As was the custom, Tubman's mother was directed to be a cook for another family, which separated her from her own family. This put the responsibility for taking care of the remaining children (a baby and a brother) on Tubman. When she was about five years old, Tubman was hired out to a Miss Susan as a nursemaid. Her responsibility was keeping watch over her mistress's baby when sleeping. Whenever the child woke up and cried, Tubman would be held responsible.

One particular day, the little girl was lashed five times in the morning. She lived with such scars throughout her life until she died. Over time, she found effective methods that helped her minimize the maltreatment meted out to her. On one occasion, she ran away from home for five days. Sometimes, she wore multiple layers to protect herself from merciless beatings. When she could, she fought back.

She also worked for James Cook, a planter. She had the responsibility of checking the muskrat traps the planter had previously set in nearby bushes. Even measles didn't stop her from checking the muskrat traps regularly. However, when her condition deteriorated, Cook sent her back to her former owner, Brodess. It was then that her mother took care of her until she regained her health. Tubman was hired out to another master after her recuperation.

The details of Tubman's date of birth are unknown due to a lack of accurate records. Some put her date of birth as 1820, while 1822, 1825, and 1825 have all been reported as her year of birth by different sources. She was an American humanitarian, an abolitionist, a trained spy and an armed scout for the U.S. during the destructive Civil War some centuries ago.

Harriet was born a slave. She escaped from slavery in 1849 and led about 13 missions to support her ambition of releasing 70 enslaved people from slavery. She made extensive use of safe houses that were referred to as the Underground Railroad. She equally leveraged the existence of antislavery activists to achieve her goal. She did all this at the expense of her life. She really put her life on the line so people could enjoy freedom from slavery.

Before the outbreak of the American Civil War, Tubman played a very important role in the lives of African Americans as an abolitionist. She was also of enormous help to the Union Army by providing assistance to them while the war was on. She worked as a spy and played whatever roles were assigned to her. Before then, what was her life like?

Harriet Tubman's childhood was not ideal. She was born as a slave in Maryland. During her transfer from one master to another, she endured beatings and whippings. Her childhood was plagued with challenges and suffering. For instance, she had a wound in the head, the result of her refusal to help a slave owner restrain his runaway slave. She was hit by a two-pound metal object that left her unconscious and bleeding. Tubman was immediately taken back to her owner, who left her without any medical care for 48 hours. She was sent back to the field in that condition "with blood and sweat rolling down [her] face until [she] couldn't see." The wound left a permanent scar on her forehead.

Infuriated by this act, her boss termed Tubman worthless and returned her to her first master, the Brodess family. Brodess made several attempts to sell her, but to no avail. She later suffered a series of pains, dizziness, and hypersomnia, which were the health implications of being hit in the head by such a heavy object. Tubman eventually escaped from Maryland to Philadelphia in 1849. She had to return to Maryland for the sake of her family and slowly helped many slaves escape from Maryland, one group at a time. She gradually moved all her relatives and some dozens of other slaves from slavery to freedom.

Despite having to make some of her trips during odd moments and through dangerous routes, it is on record that she "never lost a passenger." Tubman ensured the safety of everyone on a trip with her.

In 1850, the U.S. government passed the Fugitive Slave Act of 1850, which "required that all escaped slaves were, upon capture, to be returned to their masters and that officials and citizens of free states had to cooperate in this law." Tubman leveraged this act to help more fugitives leave the U.S. while also securing jobs for slaves who had recently been liberated so they could settle down to a new life.

At the inception of the Civil War, Tubman joined the Union Army. She first worked as a cook and attended to soldiers' wounds and injuries as a nurse. She was later handed the task of spy and armed scout. This made her the first woman with the responsibility of leading an armed expedition during a war. She was at the front during the Combahee Ferry raid, which resulted in the liberation of more than 700 slaves.

When the war was over, Tubman retired to the New York home she had purchased in 1859. It was there that she became the caregiver for her parents. She also participated in a movement known as women's suffrage until she was rendered incapacitated by an illness. She was taken to a home for elderly people of African heritage, which she had helped establish some years earlier. She died in 1913 and became an iconic figure in the history of American freedom and courage.

Escape from slavery

When Tubman fell sick in 1849, her boss made several failed attempts to sell her. This was due to the impact of the sickness on her value as a slave. The sickness reduced her value drastically and her boss wanted to cash in on her remaining value before it depreciated further. When her master died, Tubman knew that her likelihood of being sold had increased. The death also implied that Tubman would be separated from her family.

As her master's widow was making plans to sell her, Tubman took her fate in her hands. She later explained that she had to choose between death or liberty. Without mincing words, she believed that if she couldn't have one, she must surely have the other. With two of her brothers, she made her escape on September 17, 1849. Perhaps because she had earlier been hired out to another slave master, Dr. Anthony Thompson, a plantation farmer, her master's widow was unaware of her escape for two weeks. She then posted a notice declaring Tubman a runaway, with a bounty of $100 on Tubman and $100 on each of her brothers.

Due to some personal issues, her two brothers returned and Tubman had no other option than to return, too. But her return was not for long. She had other plans.

Shortly after her return, Tubman escaped for a second time. This time, she didn't include her brothers in her plans and went solo. Although much is unknown about her exact route, she used the Underground Railroad. The Underground Railroad "was a network of secret routes and safe houses used by 19th-century black slaves in the United States to escape to free states and Canada with the aid of abolitionists and allies who were sympathetic to their cause. Another underground railroad running south towards Florida, then a Spanish possession, existed from the late 17th century until shortly after the American revolution."

Thanks to this Underground Railroad, thousands of slaves made their escape from slavery to countries where slavery was prohibited. One of the most popular destinations was British North America, now known as Canada. It was the preferred choice because slavery was prohibited in that area. Ontario subsequently became the settling point for most freed or runaway slaves.

The Underground Railroad was composed of both enslaved and free blacks as well as white abolitionists. It is likely that Tubman took a route to which fleeing slaves were accustomed. That was from the Choptank River to Delaware. From there, she probably moved into Pennsylvania, which was a journey of about 145 kilometers, or 90 miles. Since she was travelling by foot, it would take her a couple of days to arrive at her destination.

Tubman made most of her journey by night. She used the North Star as her guide and tried all she could to avoid the dreaded slave catchers who were interested in collecting rewards from the government and slave owners for fugitive slaves. Most of the conductors who encouraged runaway slaves used deception as their major tool. It was what they used to avoid detection. While on the run, Tubman ran into a conductor's house where the woman in charge ordered her to sweep the house so passersby would consider her a member of the family. At night, the family put her in their cart and took her to another house with friendly homeowners. Another important factor that saved Tubman was her familiarity with her environment, especially the marshes and woods in the region.

The American Civil War

The American Civil War provided another opportunity for Tubman to work towards the liberation of slaves. When war broke out, she knew blacks had a great opportunity to work for the abolition of slavery. For instance, General Benjamin Butler had supported the escape of some slaves who were heading towards Fort Monroe. He initially treated these slaves as contraband and used them on his farm without pay. Tubman was optimistic that she could use her skills and expertise to join the struggle. She later joined a group of Philadelphia and Boston abolitionists who were heading to South Carolina. Tubman spent some time with the group, especially in Port Royal, South Carolina, providing assistance to the fugitives.

Later, Butler had a session with General David Hunter, who was a strong supporter of the abolition of slavery. The general declared that all the so-called contraband should be set free. He went as far as enlisting former slaves into the Army, especially the regiment meant for African American soldiers. Tubman did everything she could to liberate the black slaves from their white masters. She was a real leader and a strong fighter, a dedicated woman who gave her all to whatever cause she believed in.

Nicknamed Moses

The dedication of this woman to black emancipation did not go unnoticed. In both the black and white communities, she was known and applauded for her efforts to bring relief to her people. In honor of her dedication and courageous efforts to put a stop to slavery and rescue her friends and family, she was named "Moses" by abolitionist William Lloyd Garrison, in reference to the biblical Moses who led the Israelites out of slavery in Egypt. Although she was nicknamed Moses, few people knew about her mission to Maryland because her identity was kept top secret and revealed to only a few people.

Just like every other Underground Railroad conductor in her time, Tubman used a wide variety of methods to communicate with the slaves, adapting her communication method to the prevailing needs at a particular time. Contrary to the general belief that they used communication codes, nothing of that sort existed. She created different methods of communication for different needs.

When she eventually reached Philadelphia, the thought of her family preoccupied her. Tubman later said: "I was a stranger in a strange land. My father, my mother, my brothers, and sisters, and friends were in Maryland. But I was free, and *they* should be free." The thought of emancipating her family and friends kept her fired up, and she did all she could to ensure their freedom. She first started doing odd jobs so she could save money to support her mission. In the meantime, the U.S. Congress passed a law that made it increasingly difficult for Tubman to pursue her goals. Congress passed the Fugitive Slave Law of 1850, which meted out stiff penalties for whoever was found abetting escape. Even in states where slavery was outlawed, law enforcement officials were empowered to assist the government in capturing slaves.

This law subjected escaped slaves to more risks, and more of the slaves had to seek refuge in Southern Ontario, which was then a part of the British Empire under the United Province of Canada. There, slavery was abolished. This increased racial tensions across Philadelphia, as the free blacks had to engage in stiff competition with poor Irish immigrants for the few jobs available. Tubman learnt in December 1850 that her niece Kessiah, as well as Kessiah's son James and her baby, were about to be put up for sale in Cambridge. Tubman then went to Baltimore to meet John, her brother-in-law, who hid Kessiah and the two children from the slave traders. During the auctioning of Kessiah, her husband, who was already a free former slave, made the winning bid for Kessiah and her children.

While the auctioneer was having lunch, John escaped with the family to a safe house nearby. At night, he sailed with his family to Baltimore. There, the family met Tubman, who took them to Philadelphia. The following spring, she made another trip to Maryland to help other family members leave the state. It was during this trip that she helped her brother and two unknown men. To achieve this exploit, she probably worked hand-in-hand with abolitionist Thomas Garret, who was living in Wilmington, Delaware. Her family was encouraged by her exploits and with each trip she made to Maryland, her confidence received a boost.

During an interview in 1897 with author Wilbur Siebert, Tubman named some of the people who had assisted her on her numerous trips and the places along the Underground Railroad where she had stayed. Those people allowed her mission to succeed. According to Tubman, Sam Green, a Maryland-based free black minister, was of great help. She also hid in Polar Neck, not far from her parents' home in Caroline County, a part of Maryland. It was from this place that she made a series of trips to Willow Grove and Sandton, both in Delaware.

Tubman proceeded from there to the Camden area, where Abraham Gibbs, along with Nat and William Brinkley, free black agents, assisted her passage through Smyrna, Dover, and Blackbird. From there, other agents would assist her through Delaware Canal and Chesapeake to Wilmington and New Castle. When she got to Wilmington, another agent, Thomas Garret, helped her get to the homes of other secret underground agents or William Still's office around Philadelphia. William Still was a black agent famous for his role in helping freedom seekers escape to safer places in New England, New York, and Southern Ontario.

The Fugitive Slave Law made it more dangerous for runaway slaves to remain in the northern United States. This led to a mass exodus of slaves from that part of the United States to southern Ontario. Later in December 1851, Tubman led a group of 11 fugitives northward. They evidently had a stopover at the home of Frederick Douglass, an abolitionist and former slave.

In one of his autobiographies, Douglass wrote that he had to cater to the needs of 11 fugitives at once. The responsibility of financially assisting them to get to Canada rested on him, and he had to accommodate them until he could raise transport money. Although he found it challenging to provide for the needs of these black slaves on the run, he was convinced that it was Tubman's group. That motivated him even more to go the extra mile to provide for them.

Tubman and Douglass had a mutual appreciation for each other's work. Their affection was such that when Tubman's biography was still under development, Douglass sent her a letter to honor Tubman for her role in helping many slaves gain freedom. This is an excerpt from the letter: "You ask for what you do not need when you call upon me for a word of commendation. I need such words from you far more than you can need them from me, especially where your superior labors and devotion to the cause of the lately enslaved of our land are known as I know them."

At the turn of the 20th century, Tubman became more involved in the activities of the African Methodist Episcopal Zion Church while she lived in Auburn. In 1903, Tubman donated a parcel of land to the church to be used for building a home for elderly, poor blacks and other colored people. For more than five years, the home was non-functional. However, the home was opened and Tubman was surprised when the church insisted on collecting an entrance fee of $100 from residents. She said: "[T]hey make a rule that nobody should come in without they have a hundred dollars. Now I wanted to make a rule that nobody should come in unless they didn't have no money at all."

That was proof of her selfless service to indigent black people. Tubman spent her time and resources helping as many people as she could. With advancing age came the full impact of the head injury she had suffered as a slave. The headaches and seizures increased, as she was heavily traumatized. In the 1890s, she had to undergo brain surgery at Massachusetts General Hospital in Boston to reduce or eliminate this pain. Her inability to sleep due to "buzzing" and pains in her head made her approach a doctor for an operation. She was operated on without anesthesia because she chose not to be tranquilized; rather, she decided to bite down on a bullet just as she had seen soldiers do during the Civil War when having their limbs amputated.

By 1911, Tubman was frail and couldn't live by herself. Aging had taken its toll on her health. She was admitted to the home for which she had contributed a piece of land. She was ill and penniless. Tubman later got some financial assistance when a newspaper published her ordeal. Her supporters promptly made donations to help her overcome her ailment. In 1913, she breathed her last, surrounded by family members and friends. She was powerless in the face of pneumonia.

Shortly before she died, Tubman displayed an unusual optimism and calmness. She told those around her: "I go to prepare a place for you." When she died, she was buried at Fort Hill Cemetery in Auburn with semi-military honors.

Chapter 5: The Biography of Frederick Douglass

Frederick Douglass was born around 1818 as Frederick Augustus Washington Bailey. He was an African American abolitionist, social reformer, writer, orator, and statesman. He was the first recognized leader of the African American community in U.S. history. He became the national leader of the abolitionist movement in New York and Massachusetts after he escaped from slavery in Maryland. He gained fame for his incisive antislavery writings and peerless oratory.

Although many slaveholders believed slaves didn't have the mental and intellectual capacity to live independently of their masters, Douglass proved them wrong with his exemplary lifestyle and second-to-none skills and oratory. Douglass was born into slavery in Talbot County, Maryland. The plantation where he was born was between Cordova and Hillsboro. His exact date of birth is unknown and he personally chose February 14 as his birthdate. In his autobiography, Douglass stated that he had little knowledge of his age because he had never seen any record containing information about his birth.

Douglass' mother was Native American while his father was African and European. He was christened by Harriet Bailey, his mother. After his escape from Maryland to the North, he dropped his two middle names and adopted Douglass as his surname. He had little information about his mother's identity. According to him, he learned that his master was his father but couldn't confirm it and he never knew his mother. Douglass said that he and his mother had been separated when he was an infant. It was customary then to separate infants from their mothers in Maryland. On some occasions, his mother would lie down beside him, and by daybreak she was gone before he could wake up. He didn't know who either of his parents were.

After his separation from his mother, Douglass lived with his grandmother, Betty Bailey. When he was just six, he was taken away from his grandmother to Wye House, a plantation with historic undertones in Talbot County, Maryland. Aaron Anthony was in charge of the plantation when Douglass was brought in. His mother died when he was about 10 years old and Douglass was made to work very hard under Anthony.

After Anthony's death, Douglass was taken from the plantation and given to Thomas Auld's wife, Lucretia Auld. His new mistress then sent him to Hugh Auld, Thomas' brother, in Baltimore. Douglass's life improved a bit when he got to Baltimore. His master's wife was a Northerner, and the Northern masters had a reputation for treating their slaves better than their Southern counterparts. When Douglass was 12 years old, his master's wife began teaching him the alphabet. Douglass later described the woman as a perfect example of how a human should treat another human.

However, his master wasn't comfortable with the teaching. He believed literacy would make it difficult for them to control their slaves, who may eventually desire freedom. That was the turning point in the way Douglass was treated. His master's wife stopped the education and Douglass had to teach himself how to read and write, learning from the children in the neighborhood when he could. Secretly, he read pamphlets, newspapers, political materials, and any kind of writing he could lay his hands on. This proved his master right. The more Douglass read, the more he began to question and condemn slavery.

One of the materials that had the greatest impact on him was The Columbian Orator. Douglass discovered this anthology when he was 12 and learnt a great deal from it. The book changed his views about fundamental human rights and freedom. It laid things bare and Douglass assimilated everything he learnt from that book. The book was written in simple English and contained speeches, essays, and dialogues to aid students in improving their reading and grammar.

Later in his life, Douglass was hired out to another slave master, William Freeland. With his new master, he extended his knowledge to the other slaves with whom he worked on the plantation, teaching them how to read the part of the Bible known as the New Testament during Sunday school. As more slaves got wind of this opportunity, the interest among slaves to become literate increased. Douglass had an average of 40 slaves who were interested in reading every week. For the next six months, they carried out their teaching and learning secretly.

When Freeland later found out, however, he was unperturbed about the activities of the slaves. The other slave masters did not share his sentiment. They vehemently opposed the idea of having literate slaves. On a fateful Sunday, these disgruntled masters barged in on the slaves during a learning session and dispersed them with stones and clubs. That was the end of the literacy class. However, Douglass's impact on his fellow slaves remained permanent.

Some years later, in 1833, Thomas Auld approached Hugh and took Douglass away from him as a punishment for Douglass's antislavery activities. He then sent Douglass to Edward Covey, a slave trader who was commonly regarded as a slave breaker – a "first rate hand at breaking young Negroes". He proved his reputation by regularly whipping Douglass. The beating was so intense that Douglass was nearly broken psychologically. However, the 16-year-old slave had another idea.

Rather than allow this slave owner to break him, Douglass used the best tool at his disposal – he rebelled. He stood against his master and defied any form of beating. During a physical confrontation, he fought off one of Covey's cousins before he engaged Covey himself in an almost two-hour fight. Douglass gained the upper hand over his master in the confrontation. That was the last time Covey tried to beat the young black slave.

From slavery to freedom

Life as a slave wasn't convenient for Douglass. Just like every other slave, he wasn't content with his maltreatment. To escape the inhumane treatment at the hands of the slave traders, he made his first attempt to escape from his master, Freeland, who had taken him from Colonel Lyold, his owner. When that failed, Douglass made a second attempt at escape from the notorious slave master in 1836. That attempt was unsuccessful, too.

A year later, he met a free black woman, Anna Murray, in Baltimore. Despite Anna being five years his senior, Douglass fell in love with her. Anna's free status further strengthened Douglass' belief that he could become a free man. Finally, he made his escape on September 3, 1838 by boarding a train heading to the Northern cities from the newly merged railroad consisting of Wilmington, Philadelphia, and Baltimore. He later reached Maryland. Although he was still some 20 miles away from the free state of Pennsylvania, he found it easier to make it to Delaware from his present location.

Douglass used a perfect decoy that made it possible and convenient for him to hide his identity. He dressed up as a sailor by wearing a uniform Anna gave him. She also gave him some money to facilitate his escape. He used this money to take care of his travelling expenses. Douglass also carried protection and identification papers he had obtained from an African American seaman.

He used his new identity to cross the Susquehanna River to Perryville. From there, he continued his journey to Delaware by train. Douglass used a series of transportation methods to arrive at the house of David Ruggles, a noted abolitionist. The entire journey from slavery to freedom across different paths took him less than 24 hours. Expressing his feelings when he became a free man, Douglass confided in a friend that he felt as if he just had a narrow escape from a den of hungry lions.

Once he arrived at his destination, Douglass sent for Anna to join him in New York. Anna came along with the basic things they needed to start a home. On September 15, 1838, they were married by a black minister, exactly 12 days after Douglass arrived in New York. To become anonymous and divert undue attention from themselves, they took Johnson as their married name and moved to New Bedford, Massachusetts, where they settled down. It was in New Bedford that they had their children.

Douglass tried to earn a living and support his family by doing menial jobs. He got involved with the antislavery moment that was gaining momentum in the North at that time. In 1841, he attended a meeting of abolitionists in Nantucket, Massachusetts, where he delivered a touching speech that was centered on his experience as a slave. The Massachusetts Antislavery Society hired him to use his story to encourage other slaves at abolitionist meetings. Douglass later became a well-known anti-slavery lecturer. His story impressed William Lloyd Garrison, the founder of The Liberator, so much that Garrison wrote about Douglass in one of his articles. Some days after the story, Douglass had an opportunity to deliver his first anti-slavery speech at the annual convention of the Massachusetts Anti-Slavery Society held in Nantucket.

After his first autobiography was published in 1845, Douglass travelled overseas to evade recapture by those after him. He sailed to Liverpool and got to Ireland at the inception of the Potato Famine. For two years, he lived in Britain and Ireland, addressing huge crowds on the negative impact of slavery. His addresses were so powerful, some facilities used for the lectures were crowded beyond imagination. He later admitted that the British did not treat him based on his skin color but, rather, as a man.

During the whole time, some of his British supporters, led by the indefatigable Anna Richardson, raised funds to buy Douglass's freedom from Thomas Auld, his slave master, so that he could become legally free in the U.S. Although many of his supporters encouraged him to settle down in England, the presence of his wife in Massachusetts and the lives of more than three million black Americans in bondage throughout the United States got the better of him and influenced Douglass's decision. He later returned to the U.S. in 1847 as a free man.

Some of the abolitionist newspapers he produced upon his return to the U.S. were the Frederick Douglass Weekly, The North Star, and Frederick Douglass' Paper. Others were the New National Era and Douglass' Monthly. He expressed his belief in The North Star motto. The motto was "Right is of no Sex – Truth is of no Color – God is the Father of us all, and we are all brethren."

Douglass delivered an epic address on July 5, 1852 to a cross-section of women who were members of the Rochester Anti-Slavery Sewing Society. The speech became so powerful, it was later referred to as "What to the slave is the 4th of July?" In this speech that was given on the anniversary of the second day of the United States' independence, Douglass analyzed the argument made by the government against the slave trade in the U.S. According to Douglass, the government's mention of citizenship, liberty, and freedom did not reflect the real United States. He considered that a slap in the face for the millions of people in the United States who were still in slavery. He claimed that such individuals lacked liberty, freedom, and citizenship, which ought to be the essence of Independence Day.

In addition to the continued enslavement of some African Americans, Douglass also frowned at how the enslaved people were subjected to merciless exploitation and other inhumane treatment, such as torture and cruelty. He also believed in the use of education as a powerful tool to improve an average African American's life. This was responsible for his advocacy for school desegregation. Douglass realized that the teaching facilities in New York and the instructions for teaching African American children could not compete with those used for whites. He appealed to the court to make all schools open to all children without any form of segregation. Douglass was of the opinion that improved education was more important for illiterate African Americans than some less relevant issues like suffrage.

Women's rights

Douglass wasn't interested only in slave emancipation. He was equally concerned about the gender discrimination women faced. He eventually took it upon himself to become an advocate of women's rights. When the first session of the women's rights convention was held in New York in 1848, Douglass was the only black man in attendance. When it was time for the assembly to decide the objective of women's suffrage as raised by Elizabeth Cady Stanton, most in attendance were against the idea. However, Douglass spoke in favor of the idea and argued that he wouldn't accept the opportunity to vote if women were deprived of the same privilege. His speech had so much impact on the resolution, the idea was subsequently sanctioned.

The Civil War and Reconstruction

Douglass was already one of the most famous Americans of African descent when the Civil War broke out. He leveraged his status and fame to influence the huge role African Americans played in the war. He met with President Abraham Lincoln in 1863 regarding the issue of how black soldiers were treated. He insisted that African Americans deserved a place in the Civil War. His argument was that slaves would be fighting for their personal interest: freedom.

Due to the persistence of Douglass, President Lincoln ordered the recruitment of African Americans to join the Union army. During the course of the war, Douglass never relented in his efforts to get better treatment for the black soldiers. Each of his meetings with the president led to upgraded roles for the black fighters. That increased the efficiency of the fighters during the war.

Although Douglass improved the status of black soldiers during the war and worked towards the liberation of blacks from slavery, his fight was not over. The year of Reconstruction was another test of his dedication to the

African cause. Although slavery was history, another wave of discrimination swept through the country. Racism became the modern slavery. Blacks faced severe discrimination. Some people went so far as to seek a court injunction that would overturn the law that liberated the black slaves.

Douglass began to publish a newspaper, New National Era, with his sons. He published the newspaper in Washington, D. C. and used it to show his support for racial equality, not discrimination. Later, he met with another U.S. president, Andrew Johnson, to discuss the issue of black suffrage – the right of black people to vote. Douglass was of the opinion that because black people had fought for the Union in the Civil War, they deserved the chance to vote.

On January 1, 1863, the Emancipation Proclamation of President Lincoln took effect. The proclamation offered freedom to all slaves in the Confederacy. In the 1864 election, Douglass opposed Lincoln due to Lincoln's inability to publically endorse suffrage for free African American men. However, the Thirteenth Amendment to the Constitution led to the eradication of slavery throughout the United States. That was a welcome relief for the millions of slaves throughout the country.

Douglass received several political appointments after the Civil War. He once served as the Freedman's Savings Bank's president and as the Dominican Republic's charge d'affaires. When he wasn't comfortable with some policies of the U.S. government, Douglass resigned from his ambassadorial position. After his resignation, he was appointed consul-general and minister-resident to the Republic of Haiti. He held this post for two years, between 1889 and 1891.

In 1872, Douglass was nominated as the running mate for Victoria Woodhull during the presidential election. The nomination of Douglass was a big surprise to him. He was unaware of the nomination, and it was done without his consent. As a result, he didn't campaign for the election. However, his nomination was a landmark achievement for blacks in America. It was an unprecedented achievement in the history of the U.S. to have an African American on the presidential ballot.

On February 20, 1895, Douglass died of a stroke or heart attack shortly after he returned from a meeting of the National Council of Women in Washington. He was given a befitting burial at Mount Hope Cemetery in New York. During his lifetime, Douglass contributed significantly to the emancipation of blacks and used all his power and resources to ensure that blacks got equal treatment compared to their white counterparts.

Chapter 6: The Civil War and the Role of African Americans

Apart from the Revolutionary War, another war in which African Americans played a significant role was the American Civil War. This includes hundreds of thousands of free black soldiers who fought in the war along with more than four million slaves who proved their mettle as well. These fighters composed 14 percent of the U.S. population at the time the war broke out. They served the country as soldiers in the Confederate and Union armies.

The American Civil War was a four-year war between the U.S. and 11 Southern states that had formed the Confederate States of America after seceding from the U.S. When the Civil War broke out in 1861, neither the South nor the North sanctioned the enlistment of slaves in their militaries. The only concession was the use of those slaves as laborers during the war, as they were not considered good enough for combat. The resistance to their enlistment came from all quarters: the low-level fighters in the U.S. army to the politicians controlling the country to the powerful generals controlling the Army. They believed that training black slaves in warfare, arming them, and assigning them military ranks, was tantamount to publicly admitting that these slaves were of equal importance to whites. They were against any policy that would give slaves civil equality to blacks.

Although the Civil War was fought with emancipation in mind, a large number of Northerners couldn't imagine fighting beside black fighters. As a result of this discrimination, the number of black fighters was below what was expected. On the other hand, the Navy was a bit more accommodating than the Army. In the Navy, a good number of African Americans used their skills to fight on behalf of America.

In the Union Navy

The Union Navy was the alias given to the American Navy while the Civil War was ongoing. Black men were prevented from joining the United States Army by the Militia Acts of 1792. The U.S. Army adhered to this act until a year into the Civil War. However, such a policy was never adopted by the Navy. Blacks were limited because only five percent could serve in the Army in the 1840s. Both before the war and after it, white and black men were together in the Army.

Prior to the war, hundreds of African Americans served in the Navy. After the capture of Fort Sumter, that number increased, as many black people decided to join the U.S. Navy. When the war started in 1861, only six percent of the Navy was black, but the situation changed in 1862 when there was a surge in the number of African Americans in the Navy; their numbers rose to 15 percent. A good number of blacks who joined the Navy came from the East Coast. Many of them were veteran sailors, while some others had worked in different occupations in the shipping industry. The largest percentage came from the Chesapeake area and Maryland.

Every important naval battle and major campaign had some African American fighters. These black fighters fought fearlessly in the blockading squadrons and gulf coasts during the war. In recognition of their distinct roles, eight African American fighters were awarded the U.S.'s highest honor, the Congressional Medal of Honor. African American women also contributed to the war. Most of them served as nurses on the USS Red Rover, which was a hospital ship stationed on the Mississippi River.

In the Union Army

President Abraham Lincoln was afraid of having black men in the U.S. army. He feared blacks would crave secession if former or escaped slaves were armed. He thought the situation on the ground would be negatively impacted if such an event occurred. However, after two years the president changed his mind. He reconsidered his stance when he realized the North needed more fighters, as it was faring badly. More hands were needed by most of the regiments if the Union was to have a chance of winning the war.

The Militia Act of 1862 allowed African Americans to be used as laborers but not soldiers. Although blacks were not allowed into the Army, they formed a couple of militia units to support the Army whenever there was a need for their assistance. New Orleans had three such militia groups. These were the Louisiana Native Guard groups, which were later integrated into the U.S. Army as the 73rd to the 75th U.S. Colored Infantry.

Kansas also formed the First Kansas Colored Infantry. This unit was absorbed by the U.S. Army and became the 79th U.S. Colored Infantry. This unit fought a great battle at Island Mound in Missouri towards the end of 1862. The same was witnessed in South Carolina. In November 1862, the First South Carolina Infantry, African Descent was formed and later became incorporated into the Army as the 33rd U.S. Colored Infantry. By January 1863, all these units had been integrated into the U.S. Army and became known as the Union Army.

The 54th Massachusetts Infantry Regiment was perhaps the most famous of these units. In February 1863, John Albion Andrew, the Massachusetts governor, made the initial opening for African American soldiers to join the U.S. Army, thus leading to an influx of African Americans into the U.S. Army. More than 1,000 African Americans responded to his call and joined the Army. Some of them came from long distances, including Canada and the Caribbean. The governor selected a Caucasian officer named Robert Gould Shaw to lead them.

The statistics at the end of the war showed that African Americans played a significant role in the war. For instance, almost 180,000 black men enlisted in the Union Army. That was one out of every 10 U.S. soldiers who participated in the war. The navy also had about 20,000 African American fighters within its ranks. Almost 40,000 of these black soldiers died, 25 percent of them due to infections or diseases.

Ten people stood out from the list of thousands of black men who fought on both sides during the Civil War. These individuals contributed significantly to the war after they received approval to take part. These 10 war veterans of African descent are:

Andrew Cailloux

Andrew Cailloux started his life as a slave. He was born in slavery in 1825 and got his freedom when he was 21. Not long after his freedom, the New Orleans Afro-French community saw high potential in him and he became their leader. Cailloux became a member of the 1st Louisiana Native Guard under the Union. He was appointed the company's captain. The efficiency of this company made it one of the best in the regiment.

General Banks embarked on an attack on the Confederate position at Port Hudson on May 27, 1863. The assault was spearheaded by Cailloux's company. It was a suicide mission due to some flaws in their plan and the huge fortification around the Confederate troops. Despite the huge losses the company recorded, Cailloux still inspired the solders not to retreat but to forge ahead in the battle. He personally spearheaded the charges. In the process, he lost his arm to cannon fire.

One would have thought the experience of losing his arm would have discouraged him. Rather, Cailloux continued his assault until an artillery shell terminated his life. He displayed such heroism that he became the reference point for perseverance and dedication. His funeral was attended by thousands of black men which later inspired many into enlisting in the Army. His bravery and exploits during the war spoke for him.

Robert Smalls

Roberts Smalls was born into slavery, too. He later worked in the Charleston harbor as a pilot. During the initial stage of the Civil War, he was given the assignment of being in charge of the CSS Planter, which was an armed military transport that belonged to the Confederates. This machine was well armed and combat ready. While the officers of the Planter were asleep ashore, Smalls stole the boat.

After stealing the boat, he disguised himself and impersonated the captain. To make his escape easy and possible, he gave the secret signals that allowed him to successfully take the Planter away from the shore. All five Confederate forts in charge of the port's security were unaware of the actions of this pirate. He later surrendered himself and the ship (along with the codebook he used) to the Union vessels on parade.

Because the Port Royal's Union commander was impressed by his skills, he recommended Smalls to President Lincoln and persuaded the president to make room for African Americans in the Union Army. Smalls was subsequently allowed to take charge of his former vessel, which was now under the control of the Union. Thus, Smalls became the first African American naval captain during the war. While he was still a slave, he had helped some of his masters plant mines. During the war, with his new status, he helped the Army deactivate those mines. He also helped destroy many railroad bridges. To crown all his efforts, Robert Smalls became a member of Congress after the war.

William Jackson

When the war broke out, Jackson was still a slave. However, he was privileged to have some power he could exploit. His master was Jefferson Davis, the Confederate president. This gave Jackson the necessary qualifications to serve as a spy for the Union Army. Fortunately, Davis did not consider Jackson a threat. Rather, he considered him a harmless piece of furniture in his home.

Therefore, it was easy for Jackson to eavesdrop on Davis and other political and military leaders. When he changed his allegiance in 1861, Jackson had valuable information at his fingertips. He readily gave the information to the Union. The information included military strategy, supply routes, and the supply shortages the Confederates was experiencing.

William Carney

Carney was another important contributor to the Civil War. Although he wasn't a free man when the war broke out, he used the Underground Railroad to escape and join the Union Army. While the Battle of Fort Wagner was underway, Carney and his regiment were in charge of an assault that would take them to the other side of the beach where the enemy army was encamped.

When the African American in charge of the regiment was killed, Carney immediately replaced him, picked up the flag, and took leadership of the regiment. By the time the Union got to the walls and took over the regiment, Carney was the last man standing and got shot twice.

The injury forced him to take a leave. He later joined another advancing regiment. Carney was shot a third time while with the new regiment. On his way to the hospital, he passed off the Union flag to a member of the regiment. It was after he passed the flag to another soldier that others realized he hadn't allowed the flag to touch the ground even after being shot three times. Carney's heroism earned him the Medal of Honor; he was the first African American to receive that award.

Aaron Anderson

Aaron Anderson is another member of the elite group of African Americans who received the Medal of Honor. He joined the Navy at age 53 in 1863. His heroic actions made him a favorite member of the U.S. Navy, their poster boy. Just two years after joining the Navy, he was on a mission to attack the Confederate forces stationed in Mattox Creek in Virginia. He took control of a small boat with a howitzer for attacking the Confederate forces while embarking on the mission. His crew located about three enemy ships that had been abandoned, then destroyed the ships when they were attacked by the Confederate soldiers who were on the shore.

They came under such intense fire from the Confederate soldiers that their only musket and a good number of their oars were destroyed. Their boat was heavily damaged, too. The crew members and Anderson managed the few oars they had and scampered to safety while under stiff attack. Due to Anderson's bravery and fearlessness, only one member of his crew was injured. That earned him a Medal of Honor.

Powhatan Beaty

Beaty was a Medal of Honor recipient, too, the third on this list. Despite being born into slavery, he was a free man when the war broke out. By April 1861, he was in Cincinnati. During the Battle of Richmond, the Confederates gained an upper hand, which became a source of concern for the inhabitants of this city. They were living in fear of being attacked by the 400 Confederate soldiers. As a result, all able-bodied men, including Beaty, were forced to build defenses for their town.

Despite being an unarmed unit, those men worked for 15 days to fortify their city and homes in anticipation of the Union's arrival. Beaty eventually enlisted in the first black unit in Ohio in 1863. Within 48 hours, he had become a sergeant with 47 men at his command. He was promoted to a first sergeant when the Battle of Chaffin's Farm broke out on September 29, 1864. During a mission that was later aborted, Beaty defied the attack from enemy soldiers to retrieve a flag some 1,800 feet away. No soldier above his rank survived the mission from his company.

Without wasting time, Beaty took charge of the remaining members of the company and led a second charge on the Confederates. This time, he forced the Confederates into a retreat. For his exploits, he was awarded the Medal of Honor on April 8, 1865.

Alexander Thomas Augusta

Alexander's heroism during the war was subtle. Unlike most men of his time, he didn't face the barrel of an enemy soldier. Rather, it was his determination in the face of stiff oppression as one of the war's surgeons that made him one of the greatest African Americans who participated in the war. His parents were already free when he was born in 1825. In 1850, Augusta enrolled in medical school. When he was through with his training, he enrolled in the Union Army. He carved a niche for himself by becoming the only colored physician out of the eight surgeons who eventually enlisted in the Army during the war. He was later promoted to the rank of major and thus became the highest ranking black man in the Army at the time.

Despite giving his best during the war, people never liked him. Twice, he was the subject of mob attacks in Washington and Baltimore. His subordinates, two white surgeons, were not comfortable having a black boss. This influenced the president's decision to transfer Augusta to Washington. In spite of the barrage of prejudice against him, Augusta did not quit his profession, and he saved lives until the war ended. He also used his position to advance the cause of blacks, fighting for their rights during and after the war. One of the areas in which he used his position was the fight for blacks to be able to ride streetcars.

Miles James

Miles James was born in 1829 and enlisted in the Army when he was 35 years old, in 1864. He was a corporal in the 36th Colored Regiment and a member of Company B. On

September 30, 1864, he was one of the thousands of soldiers who fought at the famous Battle of Chaffin's Farm. While the battle was underway, Miles was shot and his arm mutilated. In spite of the urge to retreat and go for immediate amputation, he went ahead to lead his men, using just one arm to load his weapon. His citation confirmed this. It reads: "Having had his arm mutilated, making immediate amputation necessary, he loaded and discharged his piece with one hand and urged his men forward, this within 30 yards of the enemy's works." What a valiant soldier! He was later honorably dismissed due to his disability, but not until he had proven himself a competent soldier, regardless of color.

James Daniel Gardner

Gardner served in the 36th Colored Regiment as a private member of Company I. He was also one of the black soldiers in action at the Battle of Chaffin's Farm.

His regiment was among several consisting of black troops assigned to launch an attack on the Confederates at New Market Heights. His company was under Brigadier General John Gregg. The mission turned out to be a serious one, as his company was met with intense fire from the Confederates, leading to the death, capture, or maiming of more than half the black troops. During this bloody attack, Gardner saw one of the Confederate officers gathering his men on the parapet. He used the opportunity to charge ahead of his unit, shoot the Rebel officer, and kill him with his bayonet. The following day, Gardner was promoted to sergeant and received a Medal of Honor for such an exemplary display of courage and leadership in the face of danger.

John Lawson

John Lawson was born on June 16, 1837. He was a perfect example of the extent to which some people can endure pain to achieve their goal. He enlisted in the Army when he was 28. His assignment took him to the USS Hartford. His team was an ammunition team and he had the responsibility of supplying the deck guns.

On August 5, 1863, during the Battle of Mobile Bay, a Confederate shell maimed Lawson. He was the only surviving member of his team and his leg was badly injured after he had been thrown against the side of a ship. After he regained his composure, Gardner defied all entreaties to go for medical treatment. With just one leg, he continued his task, which had previously been handled by six men. He received a Medal of Honor for his efforts there.

In all, 25 African Americans were singled out for the Medal of Honor while the Civil War was underway. The breakdown includes seven members of the Union Navy and 15 members of the United States Colored Troops. The other soldiers were attached to army units. Fourteen of these recipients were rewarded for the role they played during the destructive Battle of Chiffin's Farm, where black soldiers faced stiff opposition. Four other men also won Medals of Honor in recognition of their exploits at the Battle of Mobile Bay. These gallant soldiers contributed either directly or indirectly to the Civil War.

William Harvey Carney's efforts during the Civil War made him the first African American to deserve the award. However, it was Robert Blake who received the first award. Blake received his Medal of Honor in 1864, while Carney had to wait until 1900 before he received his. It wasn't unusual for this prize to be awarded to the recipient decades after the end of the conflict. In one case, Andrew Jackson Smith received his medal in 2001 – some 137 years after he won it. This delay was a result of a battle report that had gone missing. It was the longest delay any of the recipients faced in getting their award.

Chapter 7: Jim Crow Laws

Jim Crow laws were pro-segregation state and local laws in the Southern United States. The laws were enacted in the 19th century by Democratic legislatures that were predominantly white. Some civil rights groups later perceived the laws as a derogatory reference to blacks and a potent tool for enforcing racial discrimination. Jim Crow laws were enacted immediately after the Reconstruction period and were in existence until 1965. They were based on the idea of the supremacy of whites over blacks and were whites' reaction to Reconstruction, which had assigned equality of status to blacks.

The laws mandated racial discrimination across all states that had once been in the Confederate States of America. Beginning in 1896, public facilities were designed primarily for whites, and blacks had no access to them. For instance, public education was segregated so that black children couldn't attend the same schools as their white counterparts.

Segregation was later extended to public transportation and facilities. It was so pronounced that it was effective on interstate trains, cars, and buses. Sometimes, facilities were available for whites that were not in existence for blacks. When such facilities did exist for blacks, they were usually of a lower standard than those for whites. Segregation created educational, economic, and social disadvantages. It was common in Southern states.

However, there was also segregation in the North. This was a de facto segregation enforced by private organizations and it included such aspects as bank lending practices, private covenants, and job discrimination. It also included labor union practices. For instance, despite the fact that 16 members of the Louisiana General Assembly were black, a law was passed prohibiting equality between blacks and whites. By implication, blacks in the assembly were inferior to whites in the same assembly. Throughout the Southern states, a division was established between blacks and whites. Segregation was not treated with levity.

This new law turned the rights of blacks upside down, especially a law designed to weaken black suffrage. Southern states embarked on a mission to limit the voting rights of blacks, creating stringent conditions for eligibility to vote. For instance, prior to the law, millions of African Americans could vote. With the law, everything changed. Eligibility to vote was based on several factors such as owning property, being literate, or having grandfathers who were eligible voters.

Other conditions included payment of poll taxes and having good character. Before the law, Louisiana alone had more than 130,000 black voters on record. With the application of this law, only a little more than 1,300 (representing one percent) could vote. The new policy drastically reduced the ability of blacks to participate in an election. They were reduced to second-class citizens in the country.

Jim Crow laws fostered discrimination. In South Carolina, white and black textile workers were prevented from associating with each other, even at work. They could not enter a room through the same door, or work together in the same room. Some employers even refused to hire blacks while others who already had blacks on their payrolls passed rules to remove them from their jobs. This increased the unemployment rate among blacks.

The situation was so bad in Richmond that blacks could not live on any street they chose. Blacks could live only on streets where they could marry a significant percentage of the residents. Because blacks couldn't marry people of a different color, they couldn't live among whites. Thus, having blacks as neighbors was taboo and no black could live near whites, even if he had the means to do so.

Some years later, Texas had six towns where blacks were not permitted to live. Regardless of one's status, a person couldn't live in those towns if he or she wasn't white. In the communications sector, the story was the same. According to a Jim Crow curfew passed by Mobile, blacks were not allowed to leave their homes after 10 p.m. Doors and ticket windows had signs that were marked for a specific race. "Whites Only" and "Colored" signs hung everywhere. The segregation was real and had a negative impact on people.

In Georgia, there were black parks and white parks. In Oklahoma, there were different phone booths for blacks and whites. Hospitals, prisons, and orphanages were also separated with different facilities for whites and blacks. North Carolina did not support the idea of black and white students using the same textbooks. In Florida, such textbooks couldn't be kept in the same place.

Fraternal social groups in Virginia forbade black and white members of the same organization from addressing as "Brother" those members who were of a different color. This was done to ensure that students of different colors were prevented from mingling in school. No social contact. No physical contact. In fact, any form of contact between white and black students was forbidden.

Libraries were subjected to the same laws. Libraries for blacks were almost nonexistent and the few that did exist were underfunded. They were not stocked with relevant and new books that were of the same value as the books available to their white counterparts. Rather, only secondhand books and other outdated resources were available in blacks' libraries. The result was a sharp contrast in the performances of white and black students.

Following are some excerpts from the law:

"It shall be unlawful for a negro and white person to play together or in company with each other in any game of cards or dice, dominoes or checkers."—**Birmingham, Alabama, 1930**

"Separate free schools shall be established for the education of children of African descent; and it shall be unlawful for any colored child to attend any white school, or any white child to attend a colored school."—**Missouri, 1929**

"All railroads carrying passengers in the state (other than street railroads) shall provide equal but separate accommodations for the white and colored races, by providing two or more passenger cars for each passenger train, or by dividing the cars by a partition, so as to secure separate accommodations."—**Tennessee, 1891**

How did these laws gain such popularity? The answer to this question lies in the laws' origins.

Origins of Jim Crow laws

During the Reconstruction period (1865-1877), federal laws provided African Americans in the U.S. with civil rights protection. The federal laws were created to offer former slaves and blacks who had been granted freedom before the war some measure of equality with their white neighbors. However, during the 1870s, Southern legislatures experienced an increase in the number of Democrats in the ruling group. The Democrats used paramilitary groups with an insurgent background to get their own way. Republican office holders were chased out of town; peaceful Republican gatherings were disrupted, while blacks were suppressed beyond measure to give up their voting rights.

Voter fraud was used extensively during this period. Gubernatorial elections were a shadow of what they once were, as blacks were subjected to increased violence during election campaigns, starting from 1868. Nine years later, the Southern states gained more support during the presidential elections when a Democratic party was brought by the South to give them more support. The last batch of federal troops withdrew from the South, paving the way for the official legalization of the Jim Crow laws and the official segregation of black people from the predominantly white population.

In the 1880s, blacks still had a good shot at local offices, although they had zero chances at the state and national levels. The Democrats later passed laws to increase the restrictiveness of electoral rules and voter registration. This resulted in reduced political participation among most blacks in the country as well as poor whites. The decades between 1890 and 1910 witnessed a change in the policy that eventually saw blacks lose their rights. Ten out of the 11 former Confederate states created constitutional amendments or new constitutions that disenfranchised a huge majority of blacks and some thousands of destitute whites through literacy tests, poll taxes, and other strict conditions that reduced these people's eligibility to vote.

Although the Grandfather Clauses that exempted poor and illiterate whites from the new restriction on voters gave these whites the chance to exercise their franchise, the same cannot be said of blacks. Their rights were trampled upon. The result was a gradual reduction in the number of voters, as seen in voting statistics from across the country. In 1900, Louisiana saw its number of black voters reduce drastically to 5,000, yet blacks formed the largest community in the state. Only 730 black voters remained in the state a decade later – just 0.5 percent of eligible black voters.

After the introduction of the new policy, almost half the parishes in Louisiana had no eligible black voters. Nine other parishes had only a single registered black voter. The story wasn't much different in North Carolina. Between 1896 and 1904, black voters were eliminated in that state. In essence, blacks in those areas were rendered politically invisible.

President Woodrow Wilson was one of the earliest propagators of Jim Crow laws. He was a Democrat from New Jersey, although he grew up in the South. His cabinet was filled with many Southerners. These cabinet members used their position to push for segregation despite the fact that the federal offices and Washington, D. C. had been integrated immediately after the Civil War. In 1913, one of the president's appointees, William Gibbs, expressed his opinion of the inconvenience of white women working in the same workplace with blacks.

He questioned the rationale behind having black and white women working together. He was of the opinion that white women should have only white workmates. Despite a wave of protest from national groups and a host of African American leaders, Wilson gradually introduced the segregation policy. Most of his cabinet members were Southern politicians whom he appointed because of his belief that those cabinet members would support his goal of ensuring discrimination against blacks. Wilson was of the opinion that his policy was in the best interest of whites.

Practical examples of Jim Crow laws

Fact 1: Black and white children were not allowed to attend the same schools, so they each had their own schools. Often, the level of education at the schools wasn't the same. There were also separate colleges and universities for blacks and whites.

Fact 2: The government kept separate records for black and white people, including marriages, births, deaths, and even biographies.

Fact 3: Blacks were not allowed marry whites. If two people of opposite gender and color were seen together, it became news and often authorities or families would get involved.

Fact 4: There were separate transportation vehicles, including steamboats. The government passed laws that forced railroad companies to manufacture separate vehicles for blacks and whites. There were certain cars that African Americans could not use, such as parlor and sleeping cars. There were different waiting rooms and offices for blacks. Furthermore, there were separate seats for each race.

Fact 5: The government tried to get rid of black votes by creating poll taxes and literacy tests, which were often unfair for those who took them.

Fact 6: There was separation in prisons, and the conditions were often very poor in black prisons because they were not maintained very well.

Fact 7: Public areas – including parks, theaters, restaurants, bus stops, and entertainment centers – were restricted. If any blacks were found intermingling, it would sometimes lead to verbal abuse or even violence.

Fact 8: Each community had its own housing areas, and the houses were situated away from the dense black neighborhoods.

Fact 9: Telephone companies were required to keep separate phone booths for blacks and whites.

Fact 10: Black boxers could train only with other black boxers; they were not allowed to train with whites.

Fact 11: Whites and blacks could not play sports together, including golf, basketball, football, etc.

Fact 12: Offices and manufacturing plants were required to keep separate washrooms for blacks and whites.

Attempts at breaking the law

Several attempts were made to break this law that had driven a wedge between white and black communities in the U.S. A good number of these attempts were scuttled by Southern politicians whose ambitions and mission were accomplished by the promulgation and execution of the law. Benjamin F. Butler and Charles Summer introduced the Civil Rights Act of 1875, which stipulated that people of all colors and races, as well as former slaves, should be treated the same with respect to public accommodations. They believed that theaters, inns, recreation places, and public transportation should be shared by everyone, regardless of differences in color or race. The act had zero effect on white supremacists.

A Supreme Court judgment in 1883 ruled against the act. It termed the act unconstitutional in many ways. With the Democrats of Southern extraction still in power, no other civil rights law was passed until some decades later, in 1957.

Rev. W. H. Heard waded into the issue in 1887. He approached the Interstate Commerce Commission to lodge a complaint against Georgia Railroad, citing the company's discriminatory practices. The railroad had different vehicles for white and black passengers. The company won the case by claiming to offer passengers "separate but equal" services.

Louisiana joined the league of segregators in 1890. Its law stipulated that separate accommodations should be provided for white passengers and colored passengers when travelling by rail. The new law made a distinction between "black," "white," and "colored" people. "Colored people" was a reference to people with African European ancestry. According to the law prior to 1890, blacks were forbidden from riding with whites, while colored people were not under that restriction.

To obtain a clear understanding of the new law, some concerned people hired Homer Plessy to deliberately violate Louisiana's law. Plessy's phenotype meant he could pass for white and ride any car of his choice regardless of the restriction, although his family was from France and Haiti. Because blacks and Creoles had freedom of marriage and could sit in any car, he was the perfect test case for finding the real objectives of the new law. On June 7, 1892, he bought a first-class train ticket and sat in a car designated for whites only.

Contrary to his expectation, he was arrested for violating the law, although he was qualified to board the train and sit wherever he wanted.

His case was taken to the court. The Citizens Committee of New Orleans followed up and fought the case all the way to the Supreme Cost. It was during the case that the court talked about assuring equality through separation. The rule was widely known as "separate but equal," which is a reference to the assumption that both blacks and whites are equal despite segregation. It was the genesis of all the forms of discrimination to which blacks were subjected after the introduction of Jim Crow laws.

In spite of the growing hatred for blacks, many black entertainers became popular among white audiences in the 20th century. These included notable public figures and entertainers such as Bill Robinson, Duke Ellington, and the Nicholas Brothers. The actress Hattie McDaniel became the first black to win the highly coveted Academy Award for her role in *Gone With the Wind* in 1939.

During this period, African American athletes faced significant discrimination. Opposition from the white community was so pronounced that African American athletes were excluded from organized sports and related competitions. Nevertheless, some boxers, such as Joe Louis and Jackson, who were heavyweight champions, and Jesse Owens, a track and field star, were very popular. Owens participated in the 1936 Summer Olympics, where he won four gold medals.

The Great Migration

This law and the subsequent killing of blacks in the South formed the catalyst for the migration of blacks during the 20th century. Jim Crow laws brought about reduced job opportunities for blacks living in the South. With reduced employment opportunities and discrimination against the few who were fortunate enough to be employed, African Americans migrated from Southern cities to the North in search of a regular source of income and a better standard of living. There were two Great Migrations. During each, millions of blacks moved from the South, where they were subjected to horrible segregation, to the promising North, where they found an abundance of opportunities to improve their lives.

Chapter 8: The Great Migrations of African Americans

The Great Migration was the exodus, between 1916 and 1970, of more than six million African Americans from the Southern part of the United States to the Northeast, West, and Midwest. Prior to 1910, over 90 percent of blacks living in the United States lived in the South, which was equally the urban part of the country. In 1900, one out of every five African Americans living in the Southern U.S. was residing in the most developed part of the country. When the Great Migration was over, only 53 percent of African Americans were living in the South while seven percent lived in the West. The remaining 40 percent resided in the North.

By 1970, over 80 percent of African Americans were living in cities. The migration had so much impact on the South that Nicholas Leman wrote in 1991 that it was one of the fastest and largest internal movements in the country's history. It was considered the greatest migration due to natural causes. This is apt, considering that it wasn't a response to starvation or other artificial causes. In terms of the number of people who took part in the migration, it outranked the migration of other ethnic groups, such as the Irish or Italians, to the United States. It meant a shift in the social and economic base of African Americans living in the United States, from the South to somewhere else.

The lack of Jim Crow laws and the job opportunities offered by the industrial North were too much for the average African American to resist. That influenced the decision of the black community to leave the challenges they faced in the South and head toward uncertainty in the North. In sharing her opinion on this migration, Isabel Wilkerson wrote that people's privileges were denied them with each passing year. People who could do things freely one day were denied that privilege the next. She said that people were "losing ground and sinking low in status with each passing day, and, well into the new century, the color codes would only grow to encompass more activities of daily life as quickly as they could devise them." This shows the hard life blacks were living in the South as a result of Jim Crow laws and other attitudes that impacted their lives negatively.

Segregation and discrimination were not the only problems blacks had to contend with. Along with these twin problems was physical violence. Between 1890 and 1910, almost 120 black people were lynched every year. The excuses for lynching ranged from outright hatred to the absurd. An African American could be lynched on the flimsy allegation of being "insolent." As if that was not enough, any attempt to improve their lot in life could lead to lynching. According to Wilkerson, a black person could get killed based on trumped-up charges or false accusations of violating Jim Crow laws. More than that, a black person faced a risk of attack for accumulating wealth, starting a business, or engaging in any activity that would improve his or her financial and social status.

Economic opportunities were slim in the South. The region's economy had been battered by the war. Its sources of wealth had been depleted beyond recognition. Investment in the South became insignificant. Hopes were dashed. Dreams were cut off. Without much to do, African Americans living in the region had to look for greener pastures. Thus, a migration became inevitable. Basically, in the South, anything that could positively affect the lives of blacks was considered a crime leading to punishment or lynching.

The First Great Migration

The First Great Migration was ignited by the First World War and occurred between 1910 and 1940. The war-ravaged South needed more products from the North. On the other hand, the North was under pressure due to the dearth of labor that could handle the increasing demand for its products. Because the immigrant populations and natives constituted the primary source of fighters, the North had no other option than to look to the South for labor. Blacks could not resist the North's incentives, according to historian Spence Crew.

Crew wrote that company owners in the North tried to attract blacks with free transportation, well-paying jobs, affordable housing, and other inducements that would make life more comfortable for them. Some companies in the North sent recruiters to the South to find black workers. The First Great Migration led to the exodus of more than 1.6 million black people from the South to the North. Some Northern cities such as Detroit and Chicago were the first destinations, while hundreds of thousands of others made their way to New York City. Within 30 years, the population of New York City had increased from 140,000 to more than 650,000. While the African American population in the country increased by just 30 percent, the population of New York City grew about five times as large.

Within that period, the African American population of Philadelphia and Chicago grew from 119,200 to 347,800 and from 58,100 to 346,000, respectively. That was a population growth of more than 200,000 in each case. Although the conditions African Americans faced were better in the North, life there was not without its share of challenges. Prejudice and racism was still an issue. Government policy was against blacks. Through a practice called redlining, African Americans were still unable to live in some neighborhoods and still had restrictions to contend with. How bad was the situation?

Redlining was a practice where financial services were denied some people in a neighborhood based on their ethnic or racial status. In most cases, the redlining was done without any consideration or regard for the victim's creditworthiness or qualification. They equally still had to make do with jobs that were formerly left for slaves. These African American migrants took up jobs in foundries, meat packaging companies, and other menial jobs. Some of them took up jobs as domestic servants to well-to-do men in the North.

Other energy-sapping jobs such as the railroads expansion were other areas where they found them useful. Those jobs were low-paying, dirty, and backbreaking. Yet, they gladly accepted those offered because the pay was more than double what they earned back in the South. By 1940, 75 percent of the black population of New York City was immigrants who came during the Great Migration. More than one-third of these blacks in New York City came from Virginia, and South and North Carolina.

Many blacks living in some cities and states had an unusually strong attachment when migrating. For instance, almost half of all the migrants who migrated from Mississippi headed to Chicago. The same can be said of those who migrated from Virginia. A higher number of these African American migrants chose Philadelphia as their new home. Most of the migrants to East Coast cities like St. Louis, Chicago, and Akron were originally living in Alabama and Mississippi. At least 22 percent of the African population in Chicago in 1940 was from Alabama or Mississippi. Migrants to San Francisco and Los Angeles were from the West, too. In 1940, 40 percent of the more than 70,000 black people living in Los Angeles were from Louisiana, Texas, or Oklahoma.

Chapter 9: African Americans in World War I

World War I was considered in many quarters as being fought mainly in Europe. Many people consider it a European war featuring an insignificant involvement of African Americans. Hence, they feel it had no impact on African Americans. That's far from the truth. African Americans took an active part in World War I.

More than 350,000 African Americans fought on the side of the United States during World War I despite the fact that it wasn't fought within African or American borders. Before the outbreak of that war, both France and Britain had colonies in Africa, the Caribbean, Asia, and other parts of the world. Germany also had colonies in Africa while Turkey, which was involved in the war, had an African contingent in its troops. However, the focus is on America. How did blacks contribute to World War I in America?

Segregation in America notwithstanding, African Americans played a significant role in the U.S. military during the First World War. In April 1917, America declared war against a European country: Germany. Not long after, the U.S. War Department saw the need for more fighters to overcome the resilient German troops. This need paved the way for more African Americans to be integrated into the U.S. Army. In some cases, they were forced through fraudulent means to enlist in the Army against their wishes. A few were arrested on the trumped-up charge that they were draft dodgers.

Some who voluntarily enlisted believed that the war was an opportunity to prove their patriotism, loyalty, and worthiness so that they could claim equal treatment to other Americans. When the Civil War was over, the U.S. Army released all volunteers who were not white. The army eventually replaced them with regular regiments made up of black soldiers and white officers. The regiments were later reorganized and formed the 24th and 25th Infantries in 1869, while the 9th and 10th Cavalry Regiments were retained.

When America entered World War I, four regiments were all-black. These were the 9th and 10th Cavalries and the 24th and 25th Infantries. Within a week of the declaration of war by President Wilson, the War Department had more African American applicants than it needed. Rather than discriminate against them, the Army was ready to do everything possible to draft blacks into the war. In a county in Georgia, while 44 percent of white registrants were exempted on physical grounds, only three percent of African American registrants were exempted on the same grounds.

Even black farmers were forcibly taken from their farms to be enlisted in the Army, leaving their families behind. They did this ahead of their white counterparts. That step was taken to ensure as many blacks as possible would participate in the war. Although the African American community constituted just 10 percent of the U.S. population, it provided some 13 percent of inductees during the war. It provided more fighters per percentage than did whites during the war.

Although the Army was still discriminatory in its enlistment policy, it gave black fighters more chances than did the Marines, for which blacks couldn't serve. The Coast Guard and navy offered blacks menial positions through which they contributed significantly to any regiment to which they were attached. When the war was over, they had served in different positions in the Army. Despite the technical eligibility of African Americans for different positions, the Army gave them little opportunity to fight in the war. Most enlisted blacks were given menial jobs. The four all-black regiments were given domestic assignments but spread throughout all the territories held by America.

The African American community raised such a cry that the War Department had no option but to create the 92nd and 93rd Divisions in 1917 as black combat units. The creation of these divisions led to a corresponding increase in the demand for

African Americans to serve as officers. The War Department felt it was important that segregation exists in the Army. The argument was that the soldiers would readily follow an officer of their own color rather than the other way around. This was intended to forestall insurrection and uprising, two problems that had been haunting the American forces for decades.

Most leaders of the African American community shared a similar sentiment and so decided that segregation should take place. That led to the use of Fort Des Moines for black officer training. This camp had approximately 1,250 African American soldiers. While 250 of these men were officers with noncommissioned titles, the rest were drawn from various civilian communities. The basic requirement for the camp was a high school education and a minimum of a 12 percent mark above the average score in the test by the Army.

Six hundred and thirty-nine African Americans were commissioned as first lieutenants, second lieutenants, or captains on October 15, 1917. They were immediately assigned to the 92nd Division in artillery, infantry, and engineer units. They were the first and last class to be trained in that facility, as it was shut down by the War Department soon after their graduation and departure. It is quite ironic that despite the higher positions assigned to African Americans, equal treatment was still a mirage to them. The black draftees were subjected to an extreme hostility that white draftees never experienced. White men were not comfortable saluting black officers while black officers couldn't access officers' clubs and camps.

The War Department didn't pay much attention to such issues, and it overlooked discrimination, too. Due to the protest of some Southern civilians over the existence of blacks in the training camps, each camp was ordered by the department to limit black intake to just 20 percent of the total camp members. Even when the other draftees were treated fairly, the treatment meted to African American draftees was less than ideal. It was reported that sometimes black soldiers didn't have proper clothing for long periods. Some were even reported to have been offered old uniforms used during the Civil War, while some had to sleep outside while their white colleagues enjoyed the warmth of the barracks.

It was also not uncommon for black draftees to be denied access to the dining hall and instead forced to have their meals outside, even during the winter. Some didn't have a change of clothes for months on end. The inhumane treatment was absurd. The only black draftees who had the best moments while in camp were those who were trained at the National Army cantonments. They had more luxurious treatment: comfortable barracks, hot food, sanitary latrines, sufficient clothes, etc.

From the service units, some troops were given foreign assignments, becoming the first African American troops to receive such orders. While going for their assignments, they were promised a rich reward if they showed outstanding performance. This promise was the stimulant they needed to give their best during the war. Sometimes, for 24 hours straight, they would unload ships and transport materials from one location to another along different routes. During the war, black soldiers worked tirelessly. They dug trenches, cleared disabled equipment, buried their dead colleagues, and did other menial jobs. In spite of their dedication to work and the stress they encountered, they were not accorded the respect and recognition they deserved. They were so badly treated that it was believed "African Americans received the worst treatment of all black troops serving in World War I."

The general attitude toward black fighters notwithstanding, their exceptional performance during the war was proof of their extraordinary skills and patriotism. When the war was over, African American fighters had served in the infantry, cavalry, signal corps, engineer corps, medical corps, artillery, and in other capacities. They also served as surveyors, chaplains, chemists, truck drivers, intelligence officers, and in every other capacity they were needed.

Although a good number of African Americans did not see any action because they were in supporting roles, some of those who saw real action gave their best to the success of their regiment. A typical example is the 369th Infantry Regiment, also referred to as the "Harlem Hellfighters." They were one hell of a regiment. The 15th New York National Guard Regiment was formed some decades before the outbreak of World War I. The infantry was later named the 369th Infantry Regiment of the New York Army National Guard.

The infantry represented the U.S. during the First and Second World Wars. African Americans formed the majority of the regiment during World War I, although it contained some Puerto Ricans during the Second World War. The 369th Regiment blazed the trail for other African American regiments to join the American Expeditionary Forces while World War I was underway. The regiment proved to be a valuable fighting machine for the U.S. during the war. They weren't nicknamed "Harlem Hellfighters" by the German fighters for nothing.

When Arthur W. Little, a battalion commander, related his experience as the commander of the regiment, he wrote "it was official that the outfit was 191 days under fire, never lost a foot of ground or had a man taken prisoner, though on two occasions men were captured but they were recovered. Only once did it fail to take its objective and that was due largely to bungling by American headquarters support." The regiment was simply invincible, and it consisted mainly of African American soldiers.

The regiment fought in various distinguished battles, including Chateau-Thierry and Belleau Wood. While still in action, it earned some outstanding awards in recognition of its acts of heroism during the war. One of its awards was the Croix de Guerre, France's highest military honor. This honor was well-deserved. Although the regiment made up less than one percent of the total U.S. Army in the war, it was responsible for 20 percent of the achievements of the U.S. Army.

The regiment was so successful that it became the most popular regiment in Europe both during and after the war. As proof of its versatility, the regiment is credited with introducing jazz music to France, Britain, and other European countries. Although the battalion had many good fighters, some members of the regiment showed extraordinary performance and reputation. These prominent members of the 369th Infant Regiment are:

Henry Johnson

Henry Johnson's popularity among the Harlem Hellfighters was second to none. He was a skillful fighter of extraordinary bravery. Johnson and other members of the regiment started as unskilled laborers while the war was in its infancy. He was later sent to the war to reinforce the seriously depleted French army. That was a decision the U.S. Army never regretted.

On May 14, 1918, Johnson and his Hellfighter companion, Needham Roberts, were attacked by 20 German soldiers. Although both of them were severely wounded, Johnson summoned enough courage to fight back. With his rifle and grenades, he singlehandedly held back the German troops. Even though he received several wounds during the attacks. he fought the troops until his gun jammed. He then used the jammed gun as a club to fight his opponents until the gun broke into pieces.

When Johnson realized that Roberts was to be taken as a prisoner of war, he drew his bolo knife and stabbed and slashed as many men as he could until the German troops fell back. Colonel William Hayward, the Hellfighters' commander, told the The Chicago Defender that the Germans were so confused, they thought they were dealing with an army, not just two brave black warriors who were fighting with all their strength. The Germans had to struggle to pick up their wounded and dead, and they retreated. In the process, they left behind many parts of their shirts that were riddled with bullets, as well as some of their ammunition. It was when they later traced the blood they left behind that they discovered they had dealt with only two brave fighters the previous night.

When the dust had settled, Johnson had inflicted injuries on 12 German soldiers while he personally suffered as many as 21 wounds from bayonets and gunfire. Roberts and Johnson were later awarded the Croix de Guerre, one of the highest military honors in France. The United States did not recognize Johnson's achievement until he posthumously received the Purple Heart in 1996 and the Distinguished Service Cross in 2003.

Freddie Stowers

One of the most outstanding black fighters during the war was Freddie Stowers. He was attached to the 371st Infant Regiment under General Mariano Goybet. His exploits during the war earned him the Medal of Honor award posthumously. Although many black fighters won this award during the Revolutionary War, this corporal was the only black fighter to win the award for his actions during World War I.

While he was in action in France, Stowers spearheaded an attack against the Germans. Even after he was wounded twice, he continued with his assault. He eventually died from those wounds. His men carried on from where he had stopped and eventually gained victory over the German troops. Although Stowers' recommendation was initially misplaced, an investigation into the recommendation awarded him the revered Medal of Honor.

He wasn't the only beneficiary of that investigation. Six African Americans who participated in World War II were also awarded their Medal of Honor awards posthumously after this investigation. Johnson was so good, he was nicknamed "Black Death," while Theodore Roosevelt named him "one of the five bravest who fought in the war."

The selflessness and bravery, despite all odds, that these black fighters displayed during World War I contributed in a big way to America's success in the conflict. Although they were not given the same treatment as their white counterparts and received little respect from others, black soldiers showed through their efforts that they had what it took to compete with people from any part of the world. Their heroics spoke for them. Gradually, they got the recognition they deserved.

Chapter 10: African Americans in World War II

World War II was another platform for African Americans to prove their mettle in the face of overwhelming challenges. Regardless of how badly they were treated during World War I, they once again demonstrated their loyalty and unquestionable patriotism to the United States. When World War II broke out, an invitation was extended to blacks to give their all for the United States. Promptly, more than 2.5 million African Americans registered, obeying the call. One million of them eventually became draftees, while hundreds of thousands more served in voluntary capacities. They did this to assist all the U.S. Armed Forces during the war.

Most of the African Americans who fought during the war were used as support for the white troops. Nevertheless, they pulled off extraordinary performances that couldn't be easily ignored. More than 12,000 black soldiers served in the 92nd Division; they were given a citation and decorated for the outstanding performances they displayed in the line of duty. The same can be said of the 761st Battalion. This all-black troop was given the Presidential Unit Citation in recognition of its "extraordinary heroism." Just a year before the end of the war, 145,000 African Americans were in the U.S. Army Air Force. This included the 99th Fighter Squadron, also known as the Tuskegee Airmen.

Just like the Hellfighters of World War I, the members of this group were extraordinarily brave and courageous fighters with exceptional skills. Woodrow Crocket, an 87-year-old man, was one of the Tuskegee Airmen. During the war, he served as a protective shield for Italy-based harbors, not taking his eyes from the German fighter planes that had set out to eliminate American bombers. This old soldier flew almost 150 missions in just a year, from 1944 to 1945. According to the experienced pilot, the regiment did not lose a single bomber while under attack.

Their heroic performance during the war made the Tuskegee Airmen legendary veterans in the U.S. and earned them the Distinguished Unit Citation. In addition to this honor, they received several silver stars, 14 bronze stars, 150 distinguished flying crosses, and 744 air medals. The Navy never wanted blacks among its ranks and allowed them to serve as attendants only. President Franklin Delano Roosevelt mounted so much pressure on the Navy that it had to rescind its policy and accept some blacks. However, the Navy had a policy that allowed it to relegate African Americans to segregated units. The new development did not go down well with black leaders, who accused this armed unit of implementing Jim Crow laws. The Navy had few African Americans, making up just five percent of its numbers.

Not to be left out of the fun, African American women also put on their uniforms to defend the country. They enlisted in the Women's Auxiliary Army Corps (WAAC). These black women were labeled "ten percenters" due to their numbers, as they eventually made up 10 percent of the total women in the WAAC.

Just like their male counterparts, they faced segregation in the Army. The more than 6,200 women in the WAAC served in segregated units and had to contend with harsh discrimination from whites among them. That, however, did not diminish their zeal. Rather, they were fired up to prove a point and they served the nation with exceptional distinction. While they did all they could for the country, they still had racial issues to deal with. This led some of them to compare the way Germany treated its Jews to the way America treated its black population.

Double V Campaign

The black community was not ready to keep silent about the poor treatement it received in the U.S. To champion the cause of blacks, the Pittsburg Courier, one of America's largest newspapers owned by a black man, launched the "Double V" campaign to fight for racial equality. In the January 21, 1942 issue of the newspaper, it published a letter addressed to the editor by James G. Thompson, who urged the newspaper to launch a campaign tagged "Double V." The paper launched the campaign and used the theme "Democracy: Victory at Home, Victory Abroad" in its February 7, 1942 issue.

Of course, the enemy they had to overcome at home included discrimination, racism, Jim Crow laws, and prejudice. The degree of racial discrimination against blacks in the South made life difficult for them. With their resilience, skills, and bravery during the wars, they were able to silence the voices of discrimination against them. This paved the way for the full integration of African Americans into the military. A former U.S. Army Colonel, Bill De Shields, believed the participation of African Americans during the war and subsequent wars enabled the white community to understand blacks better. He equally believed that their roles in the war showed that blacks and whites could co-exist without prejudice. Contrary to the previous opinion that blacks and whites should not work together, Bill believed that color was immaterial under such circumstances.

The objective of the Double V campaign was to encourage oppressed African Americans to offer full support for the country during the war while not forgetting to fight for their rights. The campaign received overwhelming support as people found a platform that allowed them to fight for their rights without shirking their civic responsibilities. The slogan was used to remind the discriminated-against blacks to protect the country and the freedom for which they were fighting. The goal was to fight against their internal oppressors as well as the foreigners who had the idea of enslaving them.

To drive home the point, the publishers of the newspaper adopted many techniques that boosted the support the newspaper received from the black community. The paper used photos of white people standing beside African Americans in its bid to indicate that the goal of achieving equality was possible. The paper wanted to drive home the important fact that the desire to achieve democracy was not an exclusive prerogative of blacks but would have benefits for whites, too.

The newspaper also used photos of people of different colors flashing the campaign logo. It was a reminder that winning the war couldn't be achieved if citizens were against each other. The newspaper then urged leaders to back their democracy speech with an internal demonstration. The country was encouraged to not preach democracy to the outside world while it remained a mirage in the country itself. Although the campaign was short-lived, it achieved an important goal: providing the best platform for African Americans who wanted a means to express their disapproval of racial discrimination as well as contribute to the war effort in their own way.

Other newspapers with black publishers followed suit. Not long after, the Washington Tribune, the Los Angeles Sentinel, and the Challenger of Columbus adopted the Double V campaign. In 1948, President Harry Truman gave repeated orders for the U.S. military to be integrated. However, while the Korean War was underway, until some years later, in 1953, black soldiers were still treated with disdain.

By the time America engaged in the Vietnam War in the 1960s and 1970s, African American soldiers had been fully integrated. From the highest- to lowest-ranking officers, one could find African Americans everywhere. There were black admirals, and a good number of them were captains, too. Mr. Shields was full of praise for the amazing contributions blacks made to the wars. He said: "The Vietnam War was the one war in which blacks did it all. They were the generals, they were the leaders, they flew the airplanes, they drove the tanks, they were in combat units, they led troops in battle, they did it all and they did it well so there was nothing left to prove."

Blacks did all they could to support America in different ways. They were not held back by the discrimination they faced. Rather, they overcame all those challenges to prove they had what it took to succeed. They believed that if whites could do it, they could do it, too. That motivated them to be committed to the war, and they gave their all to it.

After the war, many African Americans settled down to normal lives. They were content to enjoy life after the war. However, something else was in store for them. Another migration was on the horizon. The second Great Migration was around the corner. For the second time, African Americans had to relocate.

Chapter 11: The Second Great Migration of African Americans

The Second Great Migration refers to the migration of more than five million people of African descent from the South to other parts of the United States, such as the Midwest, North, and West. The Second Migration started in 1940 prior to World War II. Both during and after World War II, the migration continued until 1970. The migration saw millions of African Americans relocated to Oakland, Los Angeles, Richmond, California, and Long Beach. These places offered them skilled jobs that would improve their lot in life. Blacks were also embittered by the high levels of discrimination they faced in the South. They now saw this as an opportunity to accomplish two important goals: escape from the demeaning discrimination and improve their financial status.

In contrast to the First Great Migration, which was predominantly the migration of people from rural areas to urban areas between 1910 and 1930, most African Americans lived and worked in urban areas before the Second Great Migration. Their goal was to take up jobs in industrial cities and, if possible, the U.S. Army. African Americans who were the subjects of segregation and who could find only menial jobs were offered skilled jobs with better pay than they could locate in their Southern hometowns. When the migration was over, these black migrants had become exposed and urbanized. Over 80 percent lived in cities.

While a good percentage of blacks suffered unfair treatment during the Second World War, they were forced to take roles that could jeopardize their lives. During an explosion at Port Chicago in 1944, more than 200 African Americans were killed. When other blacks embarked on industrial action, about 50 of them were unfortunate enough to be tried for munity, after which they were slapped with imprisonment.

A number of factors influenced the second migration. These were as follows:

- **Economics :** African Americans living in the South regarded economic reasons as one of the factors that influenced their decision to move to the North. The sharecropping method of agriculture reduced their chances of earning a decent income. The agriculture ladder used the status of a worker to determine his worth. Due to the segregation policy, African Americans had a single job description: unskilled labor. Women had to settle for domestic services.

  Because the status quo remained unchanged for decades, blacks needed no more incentive to search for better jobs so they could take care of their families. Their poor conditions coupled with the fact that the cost of hiring black labor was cheaper than that of hiring their white counterparts, increased the demand for an African American labor force. The outbreak of World War II was another factor that contributed in no small way to the Second Great Migration. More than 1.5 million African Americans who migrated at this time were forced to make the move by the World War. Many people had to move to safety during the war, which led to the great migration both during and after the war.

- **Political disenfranchisement:** African Americans were greatly disenfranchised prior to the migration. They were denied the right to participate in any political movement such as voting or holding a political post. They were turned into distant observers in the political process. Hence, they had nothing to lose if they left the South, since the North was more promising.

- **Better education opportunities:** The adoption of Jim Crow laws by the South led to most African American children being denied access to quality education. Since study materials of the lowest quality were produced for black students, their education was nothing to write home about, while their white colleagues enjoyed the best of learning materials. The opportunity to get the best education for their children in the North was irresistible. The North gave black children better educational opportunities and they welcomed that change with open arms.

- **Collapse of agricultural employment:** Agriculture was the mainstay of the South. That accounted for the huge number of slaves who worked on plantations to boost the economy through agriculture. However, the reduction in the need for blacks to work on plantations as the war approached presented a new challenge. Blacks needed an alternative way to earn a living. The industrialization of the North offered them a good opportunity. They could work in industries and other employment opportunities without being slaves.

- **Unfavorable federal policies:** Most of the policies on the ground in the South were anti-black. From Jim Crow laws to the denial of other civic rights, blacks had to overcome formidable odds to succeed in the South. Such policies were either nonexistent or of little impact in the North. That gave blacks hope for living in better conditions – hope that was only a mirage in the South.

- **Horrible living conditions:** Blacks living in the South were living in the worst conditions imaginable. They were considered second-class citizens and had to scrabble for whites' leftovers. While walking on the streets, they had to walk behind whites. They could shop only after whites were through with their shopping. They were even overcharged for whites' leftovers when whites made any purchases. The humiliation was so much that many blacks moved to wherever offered them a little freedom from such humiliations.

- **The fear of lynching:** The fear of being lynched under any pretext by whites was another reason why many blacks no longer found it safe to continue living in the South. Although the situation had improved slightly compared to previous decades, 18 people were mercilessly lynched that year alone. Lynching wasn't the only threat to their lives. There was still extremely stiff violence against African Americans. As a result, they were in constant fear of losing their lives. One of the letters published in The Chicago Defender summarized the daily humiliation and threat to life that African Americans had to endure. The writer said: "Dear Sir, I indeed wish to come to the North - anywhere in Illinois will do so long as I'm away from the hangman's noose and the torch man's fire. Conditions here are horrible with us. I want to get my family out of this accursed Southland. Down here a Negro man's not as good as a white man's dog."

The frustration expressed by the writer mirrored the daily experiences of most African Americans living in the South. These challenges were multiplying and gradually becoming unbearable for most blacks in the South. For most blacks, relocating somewhere else was far better than living in the region. Hence, a good number of blacks packed their bags and headed north, where they had the prospect of leading a better life.

On the other hand, the North offered appealing opportunities that African Americans could only dream of in the South. They were tempted by these offers:

- **Better job opportunities:** While the South concentrated on agriculture and used blacks extensively for farming and other agricultural practices, the North focused on industrialization. With the outbreak of the Second World War, there was an increased demand for ammunition, food, clothing, training facilities, and the like. That led to an increased demand for workers in manufacturing companies. This, in turn, offered most emigrating blacks better job opportunities. Even more job openings became available when most eligible white workers were drafted into the Army.

- **Improved standard of living:** The ability of blacks to get better job opportunities led to an improved standard of living. Blacks had access to better wages and could go shopping without fearing oppression. The era of slavery was over. There was also a sharp decrease in the number of female domestic helpers. The figure dropped from 24 percent in the South to 15.1 percent in the North. That gradually helped blacks lead better, more improved lives in their new location.

- **Security of life:** One of the most important benefits offered by the Second Great Migration was the guaranteed security of life. In the South, violence and lynching led to a loss of life for many African Americans. The situation was different in the North. Although the living conditions were not perfect, there was a high degree of respect for life and there was no record of lynching. That served as reassurance for blacks that they could live peacefully without being killed by aggrieved people.

- **Better education:** As noted earlier, the education system to which black students were exposed in the South was of the lowest quality possible. In the North, blacks had similar chances of getting the best education, like their white contemporaries. Blacks and whites mixed freely. They attended the same schools and blacks used the same study materials as white students. Segregation was thrown into the dustbin of history as African American children had access to everything white children could access. Education became fun for black children, as they were no longer subjected to the inhumane treatment they experienced in the South.

- **Relative freedom:** In the South, blacks lived as slaves. They didn't enjoy any of the freedoms and opportunities available to whites. They lived as the scum of the earth and could move or enjoy life only within the boundary set for them by whites who felt superior to them. On the other hand, the North was a better place to live. Here, blacks could live the way they wanted. They could mingle with others. They had access to everything whites did. In a nutshell, they had a high degree of freedom compared to the life they lived in the South.

Migration statistics

This migration occurred in batches, as dictated by the different factors that triggered it. During the First Great Migration, only about 1.5 million African Americans changed their locations. That was due to the degree of urgency attached to the migration. However, the Second Great Migration led to the migration of more African Americans than the first migration.

The number of African American migrants lowered a bit in 1929 after the stock market crashed. Only a handful of people migrated during that period. The approaching Second World War made a lot of African Americans have second thoughts about their continued stay in the South. It was estimated that more than 1.5 million black people migrated to the North from the South in the decade between 1940 and 1950. For the next two decades, the pace at which blacks moved from the South to the North did not reduce. By the end of 1970, approximately five million blacks had crossed to the other side of the country. That eventually changed the concentration of blacks from one part of the country to the other.

During the migration, African Americans relocated to different parts of the country. From Detroit to Alaska, they packed their luggage and embarked on a journey of no return. Some moved from the Carolinas to New York. All over the

South, there was a movement of blacks in the opposite direction. This led to the explosive growth of Western states such as California. The cities of San Francisco, Los Angeles, and Oakland had a total of just more than 50,000 African Americans prior to the migration. However, two decades later, the figure rose to more than 250,000. In the 1940s, a total of almost 340,000 African Americans relocated to the Western part of the country. This was a big leap over the 49,000 people who migrated to that part of the world within the last decade.

The larger chunk of migrants to California were former residents of Texas, Oklahoma, Louisiana, and Arkansas. Within the past three years, more than three times the number of African migrants from these states migrated to California between 1940 and 1950.

During the 30 years of the migration, there was a gradual increase in migration to the Northeast. Migration to the West reached a plateau, while the North Central experienced a sharp decrease in its number of migrants. The migration signaled the end of the 30 years of black existence in the South. That also put an end to their years as slave laborers on plantations across the South. Most African Americans had already put a stop to their domestic and labor work by the end of 1950. They finally had the opportunity to enjoy the freedom for which they had fought and to start a new way of life in which slavery was in the past.

Chapter 12: The Civil Rights Movement

The American civil rights movement is one of several names used to describe the civil rights movement. This term encompasses all the groups, strategies, and social movements in the U.S. that had a single objective: to put an end to discrimination and segregation against all African Americans living in the U.S. The movement also had the goal of securing legal recognition for this group of people and ensuring federal protection so they could achieve citizenship rights as contained in federal law and the Constitution.

The movement used non-violent civil resistance as one of its most powerful tools. For over a decade, it used civil disobedience and nonviolent protest to drive home its point. This led to many goal-oriented discussions and crisis situations between the government and activists. All the arms of government, communities, and businesses had to promptly address these issues, as they exposed the challenges faced by blacks living in the United States. One of the most powerful incentives to fight for equality was the lynching of Emmett Till. After his death, his mother decided to conduct a funeral for her son, but the casket was to remain open so all could see how her son had been so badly disfigured. The response from the African American community in the U.S. was great.

Different forms of nonviolent protests were carried out in the wake of Till's lynching. Civil disobedience and protests included the Montgomery Bus Boycott between 1955 and 1956, the Selma to Montgomery marches in 1965, and several other peaceful activities. The civil rights movement in the 1960s aligned with Congress, seeking to ensure the passage of federal legislation that would overturn discriminating practices against blacks.

For instance, the Civil Rights Act of 1964 opposed any form of discrimination fueled by color, race, sex, religion, or nationalism when it came to employment. It equally put an end to the racial segregation that was the norm in the workplace, at school, and in accommodations provided by the government. Another important act was the Voting Rights Act of 1965, which was responsible for restoring and protecting the right to vote of minorities through the supervision of registration for voting and elections in communities that had a record of suppressing minorities' voice in previous elections.

There was also the Fair Housing Act of 1968, which outlawed discrimination in the rental and sale of housing to the African American community. African Americans who previously had been excluded from politics were now given the opportunity to re-enter politics, especially in the South, which was known for its stand against blacks' involvement in politics. This encouraged youth to become active members of the political landscape. The six years from 1964 to 1970 witnessed a wave of riots in several black communities, which received support from a most unexpected source: the white community.

Another important event was the birth of the Black Power Movement, which was actively involved in the affairs of blacks between 1966 and 1975. The movement was at loggerheads with the black leadership, accusing them of using nonviolence as a weapon for change but rather insisting that economic and political self-sufficiency was the only goal the black community needed to focus on. Over the years, the movement played a huge role in the abolition of discrimination in the United States. It also played important roles in other movements that ensured blacks had equal rights and were not discriminated against based on their color or gender.

Martin Luther King, Jr., was one of the most powerful influencers among all the movements that were either directly or indirectly involved in the fight against racial discrimination. In recognition of his achievement, King was awarded the Nobel Peace Prize in 1964.

What led to the civil rights movement?

The African American community did not come up with civil right protests out of idleness. They had tangible reasons why they wanted their voices to be heard. Prior to the American Civil War, more than four million African Americans were slave in the South. Those black men were forbidden from voting, while the Naturalization Act of 1790 forbade African Americans from being given U.S. citizenship.

After the war, three amendments were added to the constitution. These included the 13th Amendment in 1865. That amendment led to the abolition of slavery in the U.S. The 14th Amendment in 1868 erased the restriction that prevented blacks from becoming U.S. citizens. That automatically increased the Southern U.S. population by some four million people.

The 15th amendment was implemented in 1870 and lifted the voting ban from male African Americans. At that time, women were prevented from voting in the U.S. The country later went through turbulent moments occasioned by whites' response to the new freedoms given to the black community. Some notable insurgent movements such as the white Republican were formed to protest the government's action and enforce the principle of white supremacy. There was also the Ku Klux Klan movement. The members of this group targeted blacks for attacks.

In 1871, the U.S. Army, President Ulysses S. Grant, and the U.S. Attorney General made a frantic effort to use the Enforcement Acts to reduce the activities of the KKK. Some of the Southern states were not readily disposed toward implementing the act. Before the end of the decade, several other paramilitary groups and white supremacist groups had been established. Like the KKK and other insurgent groups, they were against the civil equality that blacks craved. They wanted nothing to do with African American suffrage and legal equality.

Although the law empowered the federal government to intervene if the states failed to implement the Enforcement Act, most of the Republican governors were apprehensive and not ready to send all-black militia troops to confront the insurgent groups out of fear of reprisal attacks leading to war. The year 1876 witnessed the disruption of the election in the U.S., which subsequently led to the death of Reconstruction. That paved the way for the withdrawal of federal troops, which inevitably empowered the South to regain more political control over all the state legislatures in the country. They achieved this after blacks were violently attacked and intimidated both before and during state elections.

To further empower themselves against blacks, the Southern states created some laws and constitutions that were targeted at disenfranchising African Americans in their states. They made voter registration nearly impossible for blacks and poor whites. They drastically reduced voting rolls so that electoral politics was beyond the reach of an average white and blacks in general. For the next couple of decades, blacks were disenfranchised, thus paving way for the Southern states to have absolute control over the region without any recognition of the existence of blacks living in those states. For over 60 years, it was impossible for blacks in the South to have their interests represented in both the local government or Congress. Their inability to vote also meant they couldn't serve on local juries in their states.

The exclusion of blacks gave whites control of the political class in the South. The absolute power they enjoyed had a significant impact on Congress. The Republican Party, which was hitherto the favored party of blacks, was gradually forced into obscurity as its members couldn't exercise their voting rights. Democrats wielded so much power prior to 1965 that the South was considered a one-party region. With the exception of some remote areas, a nomination by the Democratic Party was a guarantee of victory in both local and state elections. The opposition was reduced to a sleeping midget while the giant walked freely without impunity.

In 1901 President Theodore Roosevelt extended an invitation to Booker T. Washington to have dinner with him at the White House. Washington seized the opportunity to implore the government to make more black appointments to some Southern states to serve as a morale booster for African Americans in the South. The invitation to a black man was unprecedented in the history of the United States and didn't go well with the Republicans and Democrats who considered the move "an unwanted federal intrusion into state politics."

As the disenfranchising of African Americans continued, Democrats came up with another form of attack: racial segregation. They passed laws that promoted discrimination against African Americans. This led to an increase in the degree of violence against blacks and a series of lynchings. These were the Jim Crow laws. Sadly, these barbaric laws had the support of the federal government. This was upheld by the United States Supreme Court, which had more Northern than Southern members. That exposed blacks to more rounds of discrimination. The segregation that had started some decades ago during the slave trade era was now legalized. Blacks had to walk, drink, eat, and rest in places designated for them. Any violation of these instructions meant immediate punishment, which could be lynching, arrest, etc.

The election of President Woodrow Wilson in 1912 did not douse the fire of hatred for African Americans in the country. Rather, it fueled it, as the president ordered the enforcement of the segregation law in all arms of the federal government. The hostility against blacks was responsible for the great migrations that rocked the country in the 20th century. Yet, there seemed to be no relief in sight for the millions of blacks in the United States. That made the civil rights movement inevitable.

The civil rights movement was blacks' attempt to get the desired freedom from slavery, segregation, and racial discrimination to which they had been subjected for decades. When everything else failed, they resorted to peaceful protests to fight for their rights. Some notable African Americans spearheaded the movement. These people include Martin Luther King, Jr., Rosa Parks, and Malcolm X. What roles did these great men and women play in the emancipation of blacks from the poor treatment to which they were subjected? Let's start with the role Martin Luther King, Jr. played in the movement.

Martin Luther King, Jr.

Martin Luther King, Jr. was born on January 15, 1929, as Michael King, Jr. He was a minister of the Baptist church and a renowned activist who was the leader and spokesperson for blacks during the civil rights movement. Inspired by the legendary Mahatma Gandhi of India and his beliefs as a Christian, King worked for the advancement of the equality of rights for blacks through his use of civil disobedience and nonviolent tactics.

Very early in his career, King took to civil rights activism. He spearheaded the Montgomery bus boycott in 1955 and was the president of the Southern Christian Leadership Conference (SCLC), which he founded in 1957. In 1962, King was at the forefront of the struggle to stop segregation in Albany, Georgia. He also organized the nonviolent protest that took place in Birmingham, Alabama. A march on Washington, another peaceful protest in 1963, was one of the many peaceful protests he organized. It was at this Washington protest that King delivered one of the best speeches in American history. The speech later became known as "I Have a Dream."

For his role in combating racial discrimination and inequality by means of nonviolent resistance, King was awarded the Nobel Peace Prize on October 14, 1964. Without resting on his oars after the award, King helped blacks organize the Selma to Montgomery marches. In 1960, he followed that up by taking the movement to Chicago and addressing the segregated housing problem in that region. He later expanded his movement to include an objection to the Vietnam War and poverty. During his "Beyond Vietnam" speech, King alienated a good number of his allies who shared his liberal principles.

On April 4, 1968, while preparing for another campaign tagged the Poor People's Campaign, King was assassinated in Memphis, Tennessee by a notorious criminal and ex-convict named James Earl Ray. Many cities in the U.S. were not prepared for the aftermath of King's assassination. The riots were considered one of the most difficult episodes of social unrest experienced by the United States since the end of the Civil War. The cities of Baltimore, Kansas City, Washington, D. C., and Chicago witnessed the biggest riots. Eventually, 110 American cities experienced the civil unrest that attended the assassination of Martin Luther King, Jr.

King received many awards posthumously in recognition of his nonviolent resistance. Some of the awards were the Congressional Gold Medal and the Presidential Medal of Freedom. A day was established as a public day to honor him. Martin Luther King, Jr. Day started in 1971 in numerous states and cities. It became a national day in 1986. In the U.S., hundreds of streets have been renamed after King, while Washington State also has a county named after him. Washington, D. C., has a National Mall where the Martin Luther King, Jr. Memorial was dedicated about 40 years after his assassination.

Two important events were of great significance to the history of his movements. They were the Montgomery bus boycott in 1955 and the March on Washington in 1963.

The Montgomery bus boycott, 1955

Claudette Colvin was a 15-year-old pregnant girl living in Montgomery in March 1955. Due to her health condition, Claudette refused to give up her seat as a black girl to a white man. That was a direct violation of the Jim Crow laws that stipulated that a black man should give up his seat to a white man in public transport. Due to her marital and pregnancy status (she was unmarried), Colvin's case was dropped. E.D.

Nixon, King, and Clifford Durr waited for the appropriate incident they could use to challenge the Jim Crow laws in court since they couldn't proceed with Colvin's case.

On December 1 of that year, another black woman, Rosa Parks, refused to give up her seat. She was arrested for that. The whites considered her refusal to be a direct violation of Jim Crow laws. Nixon then planned a Montgomery bus boycott which was immediately executed by King. The boycott was a social and political campaign organized to challenge the policy of racial segregation on the public transport system in Montgomery, Alabama. The campaign lasted 385 days, from December 5, 1955 to December 20, 1956. A Supreme Court ruling that declared segregation in public transport unconstitutional led to the termination of the boycott. That victory meant a lot for black people using public transport in Montgomery and elsewhere.

Prior to that favorable ruling, King's house was bombed, while King himself was arrested for his role in the boycott.

Shortly before Rosa Park's case, Jim Crow laws triggered racial segregation that became the norm for African Americans using the Montgomery bus line. Segregation meant that African Americans could not work as drivers on the line. They were also forced to ride in the back of the busses. In addition, the law stipulated that blacks had to give up their seats to any white man on the bus despite the fact that three out of every four users of the bus system were African American.

Black passengers were also frequently attacked and shortchanged by bus drivers. They were often left stranded after their fares were paid. The hostile treatment meted out to blacks was fueled by racism, hatred towards blacks as reprisal for a previous case, and frustration over labor conditions and disputes. All these were becoming unbearable for blacks and a protest was inevitable. The arrest of Parks was the straw that broke the camel's back. It was the final assault King needed to launch a nonviolent protest against the barrage of injustices to which blacks were subjected.

March on Washington, 1963

King was a member of the civil rights organizations that organized the March on Washington for Jobs and Freedom. The protest was held on August 28, 1963. The other organizers, known collectively as the "Big Six," were (in addition to King) Roy Wilkins, Philip Randolph, John Lewis, Whitney Young, and James L. Farmer, Jr. The march was conceived to show the government the condition of blacks living in the southern U.S. The organizers also saw it as an opportunity to denounce the failure of the government to protect the civil rights and physical safety of blacks living in the U.S.

During the march, specific demands were made to the government. The demands were: eradicating racial discrimination in employment, protecting civil rights activists from police brutality, subjecting them to a $2 minimum wage, and much more. With more than 250,000 people in attendance, King delivered his famous "I Have a Dream" speech. An excerpt from the speech showed the optimism King displayed when advocating for better living conditions for the millions of African Americans living in the U.S.

This is the content of King's speech:

"I say to you today, my friends, so even though we face the difficulties of today and tomorrow, I still have a dream. It is a dream deeply rooted in the American dream. I have a dream that one day this nation will rise up and live out the true meaning of its creed: 'We hold these truths to be self-evident: that all men are created equal.' I have a dream that one day on the red hills of Georgia the sons of former slaves and the sons of former slave owners will be able to sit down together at the table of brotherhood. I have a dream that one day even the state of Mississippi, a state sweltering with the heat of injustice, sweltering with the heat of oppression, will be transformed into an oasis of freedom and justice. I have a dream that my four little children will one day live in a nation where they will not be judged by the color of their skin but by the content of their character. I have a dream today. I have a dream that one day, down in Alabama, with its vicious racists, with its governor having his lips dripping with the words of interposition and nullification; one day right there in Alabama, little black boys and black girls will be able to join hands with little white boys and white girls as sisters and brothers. I have a dream today."

This speech became so popular, it is considered "one of the finest speeches in the history of American oratory." The speech and the march played a significant role in pushing civil rights to the top of the government's agenda. It was also instrumental to the quick introduction of the Civil Rights Act of 1964. Although King did not live long enough to witness his "dream," it came true. His efforts were not in vain.

Malcolm X

Malcolm X was an African American human rights activist. He was one of the topmost figures in the Nation of Islam and used the platform to express his mind and elicit support for the concept of Black Nationalism. His admirers considered him a champion of the rights of African Americans. He did not spare white Americans his condemnation over how blacks were treated, something he considered a crime against blacks. Some detractors believed that Malcolm X was a violent man, preaching and propagating violence and racism.

Despite the barrage of condemnations from his detractors, Malcolm X entered the history books as one of the greatest and most influential African Americans. Malcolm lost his father to a hit-and-run driver. The case was believed to be the handiwork of whites as a punishment for his father's support of Marcus Garvey, a Black Nationalist leader. Driven by poverty, Malcom's mother had to cook dandelion greens for her children. A couple of years later, his mother was committed to an asylum. Malcolm was sent to a foster home with his siblings.

As a student, Malcolm was brilliant. However, hatred for blacks prompted his teacher to tell him he wouldn't make it in his chosen career when his teacher learnt that Malcolm wanted to become a lawyer. The teacher told him that blacks could not excel in that field. That sparked a spirit of rebellion in Malcolm, and he eventually dropped out of school. He went to prison when he was 20 for stealing and related crimes. There he got in touch with the doctrine of the Nation of Islam (NOI). That was the turning point in his life. Malcolm joined the religious organization in prison and continued to practice it after he was paroled in 1952.

As a member of the NOI, Malcolm campaigned fearlessly for black supremacy and fought for the separation of white and black Americans. He also showed outright condemnation for the works of King, especially his civil rights movement that promoted integration. Malcom was a staunch supporter of Pan-Africanism, black self-defense, and black self-determination. All his efforts were channeled towards giving blacks equal opportunities that whites enjoyed without fear or favor.

He promoted the Nation of Islam's' teachings, which stipulated that:

- White people are not the real people of the world.
- White people are not a source of good, but are "devils."
- White people are inferior to blacks.
- The white race will soon face extinction.

Needless to say, these teachings were rejected by a cross-section of people, both black and white. That earned Malcolm and the NOI many appellations, such as segregationists, racists, hatemongers, violence-seekers, black supremacists, and a threat to improved relationships between races. He was also called an anti-Semite. The civil rights movement had the goal of ending the segregation of African Americans, while Malcolm and his NOI group worked in direct opposition to that goal. NOI forbade its members from voting and participating in other political activities. That earned Malcolm the condemnation of many civil rights groups and members. He was viewed as a selfish extremist pursuing a personal agenda.

His criticism of the civil rights movement showed his deep-rooted hatred for that movement. He even went as far as labeling King a "chump" and considered the leaders of all civil rights groups to be the "stooges" of whites. While airing his view on the March on Washington, Malcolm called it "the farce of Washington" and never saw any reason why blacks should participate in a protest "run by whites in front of a statue of a president who has been dead for a hundred years and who didn't like us when he was alive."

While King canvassed for racial integration, Malcolm championed racial segregation. He later encouraged African Americans to return to Africa, and advocated for a different country to be created for blacks in America. Malcolm also rejected King's nonviolence approach. He was of the opinion that African Americans should be able to defend themselves against their white oppressors. He believed their self-defense should be achieved "by any means necessary." He declared that blacks had a right to be whatever they wanted to be and to be respected as other people were respected. He also canvassed for the rights that others in society freely enjoyed. Malcolm wanted his desires and those of millions of other blacks to be achieved in whatever way possible.

Malcolm had a powerful influence on his audiences, most of whom were living in Western and Northern cities. They were no longer content with the principles of nonviolence propagated by King and saw Malcom X as the real activist. They believed their wait for justice, freedom, respect, and equality was over. To his credit, Malcolm used his influence as an important figure in the Nation of Islam to change the derogatory terms used for blacks ("colored" and "Negro") to the more favorable "Afro-American" or "black."

On February 21, 1965, while making preparations to address an audience of the Organization of Afro-American Unity, Malcolm X was assassinated. The autopsy showed that he had more than 20 gunshot wounds to his arms, left shoulder, chest, and legs. Just like his contemporary King, Malcolm X did not see the America of his dream. Also just like King, the America of Malcolm X's dream has been achieved, although in a manner quite different from how he wanted it done.

Rosa Parks

Rosa Parks was born Rosa Louise McCauley on February 4, 1913 in Tuskegee, Alabama. She was a civil rights movement activist and received the aliases "the mother of the freedom movement" and "the first lady of civil rights from Montgomery, Alabama." She did not come by her aliases by chance. She contributed significantly to the abolition of segregation in public transportation in Montgomery through the Montgomery bus boycott of 1955.

Rosa got married in 1932 to Raymond Parks, who was a Montgomery-based barber. Her husband was a renowned member of the National Association for the Advancement of Colored People. At the time of their marriage, the NAACP was gathering money to render financial assistance to black men who were falsely accused of committing sexual assault against two white men. Parks took menial jobs, including working as a hospital aide and working as domestic help. With the assistance of her husband, she completed her high school education in 1933, when only up to seven percent of blacks graduated from high school.

Parks became an active member of the civil rights movement in December 1943 and joined the local chapter of the NAACP, for which she was elected secretary. She was the only female member of the group and was the secretary for more than 13 years. In 1944, Parks investigated the gang raping of a black woman living in Abbeville, Alabama. With other activists, Parks organized a strong campaign for the victim, Recy Taylor. The campaign was named the "Committee for Equal Justice for Mrs. Recy Taylor." It was so strong and effective that The Chicago Defender referred to it as "the strongest campaign for equal justice to be seen in a decade."

Prior to her famed standoff with the bus driver and her refusal to give up her seat to a white man, Parks attended a meeting held at Dexter Avenue Baptist Church. The meeting addressed the case of Emmett Till, who was murdered for flirting with a white woman while on a visit to his relatives in Mississippi. The case of two activists, Lamar Smith and George W. Lee, who were recently murdered, also came up for discussion.

During the meeting, the group received the sad news of the acquittal of the men who were responsible for the death of Till. Parks was surprised that they could be acquitted because the case was well-known and generated more controversy than the case that led to the imprisonment of the black men accused of raping the two white women. Parks couldn't swallow that much injustice in the society. This fueled her desire to work for the elimination of the rules that created an environment in which blacks and whites were treated differently.

Another event that fueled her spirit of activism occurred in 1943. On a fateful day, she boarded a bus after paying the fare. When she entered the bus through the front door, the driver, James F. Blake, insisted that she abide by the city's rules and move to the back door, then enter again. When she exited the bus to move to the back and enter again, the driver drove off, leaving her stranded. While waiting for the next bus, Parks vowed to never ride that driver's bus again. On December 1, 1955, she boarded a bus after a hectic day at work. After paying her fare, Parks sat in the row reserved for "colored" people. Ten rows in front of where she sat were seats reserved for whites.

She didn't initially recognize the driver as James F. Blake, who had abandoned her in the middle of the road after she paid her fare 12 years earlier. When the bus stopped at the Empire Theater, a couple of white passengers boarded. Some of them had to stand because the first 10 rows dedicated to white passengers had already filled up. The driver then did the unthinkable. He removed the "Colored" sign and moved it behind Park to create two extra rows for the white passengers who were standing. He then demanded that all four African Americans seated in those two rows give up their seats for the standing white passengers.

While the remaining black passengers stood and gave up their seats, Parks didn't want to do that. She stood her ground and refused to give up her seat. Years later, in 1987, when addressing this issue on "Eyes on the Prize," a public television series, Parks narrated her ordeal at the hands of the driver and her determination to resist oppression. She said that the driver asked her whether she was going to give up her space and she answered in the negative. That infuriated the driver, who promptly told her if she wasn't going to stand up, the police would be called in to arrest her. Before long, the police were called in for her immediate arrest.

While being led away by the police, Parks promised herself that this would be the last time she would ever be subjected to such a humiliating experience. She kept to her promise, as later events revealed. Parks was later charged with a violation of Section 11 of Chapter 6 of the segregation law of the Montgomery city code. She was bailed out that evening by Edgar Nixon and Clifford Durr.

When people suggested that Parks didn't stand up because she was tired, she refuted that allegation and considered it baseless. She claimed she wasn't physically tired enough to be incapable of standing. She went further, saying she wasn't old and fragile enough to suggest that aging was behind her refusal to give up her seat. She said that, at the age of 42, she was simply tired of being bossed around and was equally tired of giving in to laws that promoted racial discrimination.

The boycott

Rosa's arrest and subsequent acquittal was the recipe for a massive boycott. Nixon presented Rosa's case to a professor at Alabama State College, Jo Ann Robinson. Robinson was also actively involved with the Women's Political Council (WPC). She was of the opinion that this was an opportunity to be seized and spent the night mimeographing more than 35,000 handbills to announce an imminent bus boycott. The Council was the first group to offer its endorsement of the boycott.

The plans for the boycott were made known to the members of the black churches in Montgomery on December 4, 1955. A public announcement of the boycott was also advertised in the Montgomery Advertiser on its front page. Those who planned to attend the boycott campaign agreed that it should continue for as long as their needs were not being addressed. They wanted to continue the boycott until the bus company hired black drivers and until seating in the bus was no longer based on race but, rather, was on a first-come, first-served basis. That was exactly what they did the next day.

On Monday, December 5, 1955, Parks was in court facing charges of violating a law and disorderly conduct. After the 30-minute trial, she was convicted and fined $10 for her actions and another $4 to cover court expenses. Parks didn't accept the ruling; rather, she challenged it. She also formally contested the legality of racial discrimination.

On the trial day, more than 35,000 leaflets were distributed around the court. The handbill contained a simple but powerful message that encouraged all blacks to stay off public transportation, especially busses. This was in protest against Park's trial. Students were encouraged to stay out of school for that day, while others were encouraged to walk or take a cab to work. The protest was given wide publicity and most blacks supported the protest.

Monday wasn't an ordinary day in the lives of the black community in Montgomery. The day of the boycott started with heavy rainfall. However, the rain was not strong enough to discourage the community from carrying out the boycott. Some blacks carpooled while some used cabs operated by blacks. A good number of the black community walked various distances to work. The boycott had a negative impact on some of the bus transit companies in the city. Many public buses were idle for weeks, even months. That negatively affected most of the companies' finances. After a long boycott, the city was forced to repeal the law after a similar case had led to the Supreme Court ruling that segregation in public transport systems was unconstitutional.

In a 1992 interview with National Public Radio, Parks recalled that she was simply fighting for a good life for herself and to not be denied the good things of life, as was her experience then. She claimed that she did everything she did so she would no longer be denied access to what she was entitled to. She believed the more she refused to take a stand, the more she would be oppressed. To put an end to this oppression, Rosa refused to give up her rights. Her defiant act and the subsequent Montgomery bus boycott played a significant role in the civil rights movement in modern times. Parks shot herself into national fame through her unwavering resistance to the discrimination and segregation experienced by African Americans in the 20th century.

As an activist, Parks organized many civil rights campaigns and collaborated with many civil rights activists, such as Martin Luther King, Jr. and Edgar Nixon, the president of the NAACP in Alabama. Rosa played an important role in raising unprecedented awareness of the plight of blacks in America and the civil rights challenges they faced. In his book *Stride Toward Freedom*, King wrote that Park's arrest wasn't the genesis of the protest. Her case was just the catalyst needed to speed up the protest. He believed nobody had a deep understanding of Parks' action. It was only her reaction to what she was experiencing after her cup of endurance had run over.

When the oppression became unbearable, Parks took a stand against it. Although it was a difficult phase in her life, she did all she could to support the fight for equality for blacks in America. Parks' relationship with other activists helped her contribute in a large way to the freedom from oppression that blacks later enjoyed. Unlike King and Malcolm X, Rosa lived long enough to witness the realization of her dreams. She lived long enough to see an America where blacks and whites are workmates, schoolmates, and neighbors. Her defiant stand that fateful day was a major turning point that eventually defined the future for unborn African Americans.

South Carolina and Charleston's place in the civil rights movement

South Carolina and Charleston played crucial roles in the liberation of blacks from slavery. They also contributed to the end of segregation, discrimination, and other poor treatment blacks received at the hands of whites and the government. Here are some of the areas in which this American state and city contributed to African Americans' liberty.

When you think of the civil rights movements, Charleston, South Carolina may not readily come to mind. Perhaps you are familiar with the Montgomery boycott and other popular civil rights actions. Other notable events include the merciless killing of Medgar Evers and the tragic killing of four little girls in Birmingham. These events surely deserve a place in the history of the civil rights movement in the U.S. They were part of the reason why some concerned African Americans saw the need to fight for the emancipation of blacks. However, the story is incomplete without a mention of Charleston. This city is of historical importance because it was the site of the tragic murder of nine African Americans when a man opened fire on them inside a church on a fateful Wednesday.

It is believed among some quarters that the fight for freedom started in Charleston in 1862. In that year, a slave, Robert Smalls, spearheaded a revolt that led to the taking over of a steamboat on which he and 12 other African Americans were working during the Civil War. Smalls eventually offered the hijacked boat to Union forces. He subsequently bought freedom for himself and his family. Nevertheless, there was more to the city than the heroics of Robert Smalls and his colleagues.

Charleston was the setting of lynchings, segregation, and Jim Crow laws. Local blacks were subjected to all kinds of injustice and maltreatment that made an uprising inevitable. One of the earliest challenges the local arm of the NAACP faced was the discrimination against black teachers in the city. The district was not interested in hiring black teachers regardless of their qualifications. That led to a series of protests by blacks who felt discriminated against by whites.

One of the local black teachers, Septima Poinsette Clark, joined the local civil rights movement and used her position to fight for equal pay for the few black teachers in the city. In 1956, Clark was fired due to her involvement with the NAACP when a new constitution forbade state employees from joining civil rights movements. Clark continued in her capacity as one of the important members of NAACP and used her position to advance the cause of blacks. She later worked with the Southern Christian Leadership Conference that had been co-founded by Martin Luther King, Jr. Her responsibility was to teach blacks about voting rights. She also taught adult literacy, all in Citizenship Schools in the South. In 1975, Clark was made a member of the Charleston School Board, the first black woman to hold that position.

While this discrimination against black teachers was ongoing, other black members of the community were struggling with challenges. There was restlessness among African Americans in Charleston. Schools were poorly funded, jobs were few, and the degree of segregation was significant. The conditions were so bad that a lawsuit was filed against Clarendon County Schools to challenge its segregation policy. The jury judged the case in favor of the school and the segregation of blacks continued.

In 1962, Martin Luther King, Jr. visited the city. He addressed the black community at the Emmanuel AME Church. The African Americans living in the city were so inspired, they boycotted the low wages offered to blacks and the segregated facilities, and decried the high unemployment rates among blacks. The peaceful process organized and executed by the NAACP was later known as the Charleston Movement. Despite the protest being conducted peacefully, more than 1,000 African Americans were imprisoned for their participation.

However, one of the many stores where segregation was the motto eventually opened its doors to the black community. A typical example was the Kress department store. During the first protest, a sit-in was conducted at Kress and other restaurants, stores, and theaters that were not open to African Americans. This was in response to an owner of a restaurant who decided to make his restaurant available to the general public, regardless of skin color.

One of the defining moments in the history of the city was the killing of nine members of a black church. The Emmanuel African Methodist Episcopal church was fondly called the Mother Emanuel. The church played a crucial role in the history of America. It hosted several movements and groups promoting the emancipation of blacks. It was first used for slave revolts. During the civil rights movement, it was used to encourage members and the black community in general to fight for their rights.

Martin Luther King, Jr. visited Charleston in 1962 and addressed the congregation, urging them to exercise their right to vote. That way, they could vote for individuals who would champion black causes. This was appropriate because the church and other churches had been banned some years back due to their activities. Because Mother Emanuel was a black church, the locals did everything within their power to oppress its black worshipers.

South Carolina

African Americans living in South Carolina did not fare any better than blacks in other parts of the country. They were exposed to the same sort of poor treatment and discrimination that nearly all blacks living in the United States during that time experienced.

In the area of education, the University of South Carolina was subjected to segregation. All assistance to black students was cut while white students were given preference over black students. In terms of the economy, the treatment was the same. After the end of the Civil War, both blacks and whites became landowners. This did not sit well with politicians. They went to the extreme and included employment discrimination as an integral part of their constitution. Also, there was increasing joblessness among blacks as labor was reserved for whites.

Politically, blacks were disfranchised. The elite of the Democratic Party worked hard to ensure the disfranchisement of black voters. It all started with a notorious law passed in 1882. The law, known as the Eight Box Law, ensured a reduction in the number of blacks who were eligible for voting, from 58,000 to about 14,000 in less than eight years. When Benjamin Ryan Tillman became the leader of the Democratic Party, he promised to reduce the number of black voters in the state. He kept his word and rewrote the constitution in 1895 to suit his purpose. In 1896, all African Americans were prohibited from voting. For the next 65 years, black citizens of Charleston were mere spectators in the politics of their state.

The 1930s and 1940s witnessed the desire of blacks to fight for their rights. They were no longer content to watch their white neighbors oppress them at will. Some organizations and influential African Americans worked together to fight for freedom from slavery and segregation. At the forefront of such campaigns was the NAACP and a seasoned journalist, John McCray. They worked with other people, such as Modjeska Simkins, DeQuincey Newman, and others who were concerned about the pitiful living conditions of blacks in the state. They all encouraged blacks in the country to keep the activism flag flying so that they could use the platform to fight for their rights and effect change.

In a collective effort to ensure that black children had the best education possible, some influential members of the black community and the NAACP pooled resources to build Citizenship Schools. These schools were built in the 1940s to 1950s and played a huge role in preparing the future generation to fight for its rights. The schools were used to teach black students how to stand up for their rights against white supremacy. They were also taught about their legal rights, including the right to vote. The school also taught effective strategies black children could use to carry out effective civil disobedience. The civil rights movement used these schools as tools to champion their cause. They encouraged thousands of black people to participate in demonstrations and protests until they received their rights.

The 1940s saw the complete domination of blacks. During World War II, the state prohibited people with empty ballots from joining the Army. It was an attempt by the government to disfranchise blacks completely. The state went a step further by passing a law denouncing the mixing of blacks and whites. When the war was over, a veteran was brutally beaten by a white supremacist. The merciless beating influenced the president's decision to put an end to the segregation that was prevailing at military facilities across the country. That order was of great significance to blacks living in South Carolina.

The future started looking promising for African Americans in South Carolina in 1944. A protest was organized in that year to help blacks stand up and fight for their rights. The protest led to the formation of the Progressive Democratic Party. The party was led by the experienced and respected John McCray. Although the group failed in its attempt to challenge the rationale behind the all-white delegates who were sent to the Democratic National Convention, it made its voice heard. More people became aware of the struggle in which they must engage if they really desired an end to black oppression and segregation.

The NAACP later worked with the Progressive Democrats and launched an effective registration drive that led to a surge in the number of eligible black voters. The figure increased to 50,000 as more people became aware of the importance of exercising their franchise. In spite of all efforts by the Ku Klux Klan, more than 30,000 African Americans registered and took part in the primary held in 1948. Their efforts paid off when a candidate for blacks won a seat in the Senate over the preferred white candidate.

As they believed that education could help them achieve freedom, blacks implored the government to offer equal education for both whites and blacks. At the forefront of the quest for equality for blacks was the NAACP. In the 1940s, the group made a case for equal salaries for teachers, regardless of their race or skin color. Some aggrieved black parents in South Carolina brought the Summerton School District of Clarendon County to court, suing over the white racism to which their children were subjected in school. Judge Waring, who heard the case, ruled that segregation was an aberration and not constitutional. The judged ruled in favor of blacks. That led to a chain reaction culminating in the complete elimination of segregated schools. That was one of the many victories African Americans living in South Carolina recorded during this time.

At the start of the 21st century, African Americans living in South Carolina were able to lead happy lives devoid of the challenges that had been the norm some decades previously. They had used their protests, court actions, and other legal means to fight for their freedom. Legal barriers that limited their contribution to society were disappearing. Segregation was history. Their franchise was restored. For the first time in centuries, they could live with whites in peace.

In 1922, the first African American was elected to the U.S. House of Representatives. The election of James Clyburn to represent them in the House was the nail that permanently closed the coffin where racial discrimination, segregation, oppression, disfranchisement, and other oppressive acts toward blacks were buried.

These gains were not achieved through violence. They were the result of persistent demands for rights without resorting violence. Whenever possible, blacks leveraged the provision of the law. Gradually, federal laws were enforced to lift some of the barriers with which blacks contended. The civil rights movement across the nation and in South Carolina specifically encouraged other movements to fight for their rights. As a result, different movements sprang up. Women, people with disabilities, lesbians, and gays also demanded their rights. That wouldn't have been possible without the success achieved by the civil rights movement, which fought hard for freedom for African Americans living in South Carolina.

Chapter 13: Dred Scott vs. Sandford

Dres Scott vs. Sanford was a case that centered on constitutional law and U.S. labor law. It was judged by the Supreme Court of the United States. The constitutional law oppressed African Americans and stipulated that no black man whose forefathers had been brought into the United States as slaves had the right to become a citizen of the United States. Such a black man, according to the law, could not take his case to the federal court because he was not recognized as a citizen of the country. The law also placed limitations on the federal government because it did not have the ability to control how slavery was conducted in some federal territories that were not part of the U.S. The federal government was established after the U.S. had been created.

Dred Scott was an African slave whose master took him to areas considered free territories and states. Scott made a desperate effort to gain his freedom when he sought to take advantage of state laws that considered a slave free if he visited those free territories. However, the court decided against Scott, and his request was rejected by Chief Justice of the United States Roger B. Taney. This ruling, although not in favor of Scott, proved to be one of the landmark cases that eventually helped many activists in their fight for freedom. That wasn't what Justice Taney had bargained for.

Taney believed his landmark judgment would put to rest the slavery question that had been a subject of contention in the country. How wrong he was! Rather than settle the issue, the case aggravated it. The antislavery group in the northern part of the country did not find the ruling acceptable. This triggered dissent. Most legal scholars, lawyers, and other luminaries considered the ruling not to be a binding precedent but dictum. This ruling indirectly set the pace for the outbreak of the Civil War, which eventually took hundreds of thousands of lives. Due to the havoc created by the Civil War, the law that forbade blacks from becoming American citizens was put to rest by the Civil Rights Act of 1866 as well as the 14th amendment to the U.S. Constitution, which gave Africans living in the United States full citizenship in 1868.

The court decision in the Dred Scott v. Sandford case received many knocks from notable American scholars. Chief Justice, C.E., referred to the judgment as one of the worst decisions the court would ever make. Other notable scholars, such as David Thomas Konig, Junius P. Rodriguez, and a host of others, considered the judgment to be a deviation from the foundation of the country. One of the most outspoken opponents of this ruling was Justice John McLean. In one of his writings, he said there was no basis for supporting the Supreme Court's decision that black people could not become American citizens. The judge cited the case of five states where black men had the right to vote. This suffrage meant that the black men who voted in those states were already citizens of the states and, by extension, U.S. citizens. He therefore insisted that the decision of the judge was not really about the law. It was about the personal preference of the judge.

To buttress his point, McLean cited the Marie Louise v. Marot case that came up for hearing in 1835. In that case, Chief Justice George Mathews, Jr. ruled against a slave master who wanted to have her slave back after the slave had already tasted freedom. The judge ruled that "being free for one moment in France, it was not in the power of the former owner to reduce her again to slavery." In essence, Scott should have been free because he had already tasted freedom. Sadly, the Supreme Court did not share this sentiment. No lower courts deemed it fit to let Scott buy his freedom.

How did this start?

Although very little is known about Dred Scott's childhood, it is known that he was born into slavery in 1795 in Virginia. In 1818, Peter Blow, his owner moved from Virginia to Alabama. He took all six of his slaves, including Scott, along with him to take up farming in Huntsville. However, his owner lost interest in farming and eventually relocated to St. Louis, Missouri. He sold Scott to Dr. John Emerson, a U.S. Army surgeon in Missouri. Emerson took Scott to Illinois after purchasing him from his first master.

Illinois was a free state under an ordinance established in 1787. The state had abolished slavery in 1819, when Illinois was officially admitted as one of the new states in the United States. Under the Northwest Ordinance law established in 1787, Scott could push for his freedom and be set free alongside his family in that state. Some years later, his master took Scott to Fort Snelling in the Wisconsin Territory, which is now a part of Minnesota. Just like Illinois, Fort Snelling was prohibited from practicing slavery according to the Missouri Compromise.

While he was living in Missouri, Scott married Harriet Robinson. A civil ceremony was done by Robinson's master, Major Lawrence Taliaferro. The civil ceremony would not have been required if Scott was a slave because the constitution did not recognize slave marriages. Therefore, technically, Scott was a free man at the time of his marriage to Harriet. When Emerson was ordered back to Jefferson Barracks Military Post in 1837, his master left Scott with his family at Fort Snelling. He then leased out the services of Scott and his wife to make a profit. That act was tantamount to bringing slavery back into Missouri, a free state. It was a clear violation of many anti-slavery laws, such as the Northwest Ordinance, the Missouri Compromise, and the Wisconsin Enabling Act.

Emerson was later reassigned to Fort Jesup, Louisiana. It was there that Emerson married Eliza Irene Sanford in 1838. To assist his wife, Emerson called on Scott and his wife. While in transit to Louisiana to attend to the needs of Emerson and his new wife, Scott's wife gave birth to a daughter, Eliza. Since their daughter was born where slavery was a crime, she was automatically a free person according to both state and federal laws. When the Scotts arrived in Louisiana, they could have immediately pushed legally to be free and their request would have been granted.

While commenting on this issue, Finkelman was of the opinion that any Louisiana court would have granted the Scotts freedom because the state had absolute respect for the anti-slavery laws of free states. Rather, they decided against that. Emerson was reassigned to Fort Snelling toward the end of 1838. Two years later, his wife, Irene, returned to St. Louis with Scott and his wife. Emerson decided to leave the Army in 1842 and died a year later. After his death, his estate and slaves were inherited by Irene, his wife. For the next three years after the sudden death of her husband, Irene hired the Scotts to different slave masters. The unfair treatment moved Scott to buy his freedom and that of his wife, but Irene wouldnot hear of it. This prompted Scott to pursue legal action to gain his freedom.

Contrary to his expectation, Scott's first attempt at securing freedom for himself and his family failed. Although previous events, such as his living in free states, the birth of his daughter in a free territory, and other relevant pieces of evidence, seemed to give him a good chance at success and freedom, Scott lost the case on a technicality in June 1847. His failure to win the case meant that his days as a slave were not yet over. However, Scott didn't give up the fight.

Six months later, he was granted a new trial. This time, he made his appeal to Missouri's Supreme Court. The court fixed 1848 for the new hearing of Scott's case. However, due to some exigencies such as a cholera epidemic, a fire outbreak, and the existence of two continuances, the new trial was put on hold until 1850. While the case was pending, Scott and his family were leased out as slaves by the sheriff of St. Louis County, in whose custody Scott and his family were living. When the trial was finalized in 1852, Scott remained a slave according to the Supreme Court.

The Scott v. Sanford trial came up in 1853, in another attempt by Scott to legally get freedom for his family. He sued John Sanford, his new owner, on account of Sanford's holding Scott as a slave and for assaulting Scott's family by holding them captive for a couple of hours on January 1, 1853. He lost this case as well. That prompted Scott to take the case to the Supreme Court, where it was named Dred Scott v. Sanford. However, Scott lost that case as well. This time, the judge who presided over the case was of the opinion that Scott had no right to approach the court because he wasn't an America citizen.

This decision had many implications. Scott wasn't the only person who felt the negative impact of the unfavorable judgment. It also affected various facets of people's lives. Let's consider a few of them.

Economic consequences

The most obvious implication of this judgment was that it set the tone for the economic challenge later called the Panic of 1857. This was due to the ruling's political and financial effects on the country, as many people were scared of the possibility of slavery expanding to Western territories north of the Missouri Compromise. Shortly after the judgment, historian Larry Schweikart and economist Charles Calomiris realized there was a huge envelope of uncertainty over the West. They were unsure whether the West would suddenly lose its free-state status and become a slave territory or whether it would have an experience similar to "Bleeding Kansas" and spend the next couple of years dealing with internal crises and fighting. This led to the immediate collapse of the east-west railroads, although the north-south railroads were still running. The situation almost caused the collapse of many big banks in the region.

Political consequences

The political landscape also felt the impact of the ruling against Scott. In the South, where there were many slaveholders, the decision was seen as a deserved triumph, as it permitted them to keep their slaves and purchase more. They saw it as an opportunity to increase their slaveholding capacity, as they regarded the ruling as the best interpretation of the Constitution. A senator from Mississippi, Jefferson Davis, who later became President of the Confederate States of America, considered the ruling as helping people decide whether or not blacks should be slaves.

Before the Dred Scott v. Sanford case reached the Supreme Court, some Democratic Party politicians were already making moves to repeal the Missouri Compromise, which included Missouri among the states where slavery was prohibited. In 1854 these politicians had their way. When the Kansas-Nebraska Act was passed, each state that was newly admitted into the United States had the option of deciding whether to be a free state or a slave trade state. That nullified the existing law under which some states were automatically slave free. The recent verdict of the Supreme Court under the direction of Taney indirectly permitted the expansion of slavery into territories that were considered free states.

Hence, the decision was a confirmation of the general assumption that some powerful and influential individuals, a political party, and slave traders were pushing for the expansion of the slave trade and slavery into other parts of the United States. They wanted the practice that was previously outlawed to be legalized. In a similar vein, Southerners who previously had issues with the Kansas-Nebraska Act believed that they had the backing of federal law to practice slavery in their territories regardless of state law. Because slaves were counted as three-fifths of a person, they had the belief that having more slaves in their territories would increase their numerical power and lead to more representation in Congress. They believed this could happen only if pro-slavery territories were expanded. The North would lose its political power, as a greater number of states would lean toward becoming slave states rather than free states.

Although Taney initially viewed his judgment as the final solution to a perennial problem that had been plaguing the country for years, the reverse was the case. Rather than transform the sensitive political issue into a legal case amicably settled in court, it strengthened the North's stance against slavery. The judgment also drove a wedge between the Democratic Party and encouraged secessionists who were in favor of slavery in the South to become more daring with their demands. Finally, it empowered the Republican Party more than before.

Many anti-slavery groups and individuals attacked the ruling in the Dred Scott case. According to the Evening Journal, a newspaper published in Albany, New York, the decision was an aberration. The newspaper condemned the ruling in vehement terms. It considered the triumph of slave states over free states an offence against the principle of liberty on which the country was founded.

Although some pro-slavery individuals and organizations felt that the decision was proof of the legitimacy of their right to own slaves, many people, including the Republican Party, treated it as an attempt to make the country a pro-slavery nation. Proponents of slavery were convinced that if their rights as slave owners and the freedom to take their slaves wherever they wanted were not restricted, the future was promising. They believed they would always have their way in the issue. They were convinced that the future would allow them to auction slaves on Boston Common if they acquired more slaves than needed. They were so determined to carry on with slavery that they didn't mind doing so at the expense of the Democratic Party and the nation.

On the other hand, Frederick Douglass, an African American abolitionist, thought it was odd that such a decision could be reached by the apex court. The prominent abolitionist considered the ruling unconstitutional and saw the chief justice's decision as a deviation from the principle of freedom laid down by the country's founding fathers. Douglass believed that political conflict was inevitable as an aftermath of the decision. However, things took a new turn after Irene Emerson married Calvin C. Chaffee after relocating to Massachusetts in 1850.

Chafee was a medical doctor and abolitionist who got a place in Congress on the tickets of the Republicans and Know Nothings. Chaffee's marriage to Irene elicited condemnation from people who believed an abolitionist shouldn't have a marital relationship with a slave owner. In his defense, Chaffee claimed to have nothing to do with the enslavement of Scott since Scott was his brother-in-law's slave. Nevertheless, Chafee initiated a process that saw the transfer of Scott to Henry Taylor Blow, Scott's first master's son. Chafee's argument was that only Blow was eligible to set Scott and his family free.

Blow did not waste any time filling the manumission papers; he did so on May 26, 1857, with Judge Hamilton. By signing the manumission papers, Blow expressed his desire to grant Scott and his family the freedom for which they had suffered. The emancipation of Scott and his family made national headlines. Throughout the Northern cities, Scott's release was celebrated beyond measure. After his release, Scott took up a job in St. Louis as a hotel porter while his wife took up a laundry job to supplement her husband's income. Scott died of tuberculosis on November 7, 1858, just 18 months after gaining his freedom. His wife died almost two decades later on June 17, 1876.

In his own way, Scott contributed to the emancipation of African slaves. The publicity generated by his case and the impact it had on people made it a reference point in subsequent years. The division it caused among people helped abolitionists pull together resources to achieve a common goal: freedom. Scott's tenacity and determination to be free motivated others who were still slaves to push for their freedom, too. They knew that if Scott could be free after several attempts, they could be free, also.

Chapter 14: Black Feminism

Black feminism is another concept that has a huge impact on African Americans. The concept states that class oppression, sexism, racism, and gender identity are inextricably interwoven. The relationship between the elements of black feminism is known as intersectionalism. According to Kimberle Crenshaw, who first coined the term in 1989, it is a political movement designed to put a permanent end to sexist oppression. In the 1960s it was a popular movement that challenged the existing sexism promoted by the civil rights movement and another biased concept that was the trademark of the feminist movement: racism.

Between the 1970s and 1980s, black feminists took their activism to a new level by forming various groups. The goal was to use these groups to address the role that black women played in movements such as gay liberation, Black Nationalism, second-wave feminism, and the like. At the top of the movement was the Anita Hill controversy, which took place in the mid-1990s. This controversy put black feminism into the limelight as more people became aware of the essence of the black feminist movement. The advent of the Internet and social media took black feminism to new heights as it enjoyed significant publicity and advocacy on social media platforms in the 2010s.

The argument put forward by proponents of this movement was that black women were discriminated against in power in comparison to white women. There was a huge distinction between white and black women in power, and that eventually led to the "white feminist." This was a derisive term used to criticize white feminists who did not support the concept of intersectionality. The black feminist movement gave birth to such feminism theories as historical revisionism and womanism, which was propagated by Alice Walker. As a result of the popularity of the movement, notable individuals such as Angela Davis and Patricia Hill Collins, and black celebrities such as Beyonce, threw their weight behind black feminism. How did it all begin?

Prior to the black feminist movement, come civil rights movements such as the Black Panthers, the Student Nonviolent Coordinating Committee, and others were the order of the day. That was in the 1960s and the 1970s. The National Black Feminist Organization later realized that most civil rights movements had a lackluster attitude toward the cause of black women and decided to take up their cause. The organization was particular about their reluctance to take up some issues, such as legal abortion, forced sterilization, safe job opportunities for black domestic workers, and domestic lives. They felt that these causes were central to the experience of an average black woman in the United States. Most of the women who later joined the black feminist movement were influenced by the prevalence of sexism in civil rights groups, including Black Power organizations.

One of the most overlooked areas was intersectionality, which is the intersection of gender equality and racial equality. However, Angela Davis saw the need for that issue to be addressed and she promptly did so in *Women, Race and Class*. It was while working on an anti-discrimination law that Kimberle Crenshaw coined the term between 1986 and 1987. Crenshaw saw the need to address the impact of compound discrimination to which black women were subject. Patricia Hill Collins was another feminist who worked to increase the awareness of discrimination against women. She based her works on the politics behind black feminists as fueled by oppression and thought.

Black women were subjected to significant gender and racial inequality throughout the slavery and post-slavery eras, including modern-day inequality and oppression. A fight about gender and racial equality became inevitable as a means of controlling discrimination. The fight has many undertones from throughout history. However, many people believe that the fight for racial equality by the civil rights movement between 1958 and 1972 culminated in the black feminism movement. While the civil rights movement was busy with its fight for racial equality, the quest for gender equality was gaining momentum, too. The progress made by various movements, including black feminism, was responsible for the gender and racial equality that African American women later enjoyed. Although black feminism has some similarities to other movements, it was quite different from the prevalent civil rights movements and mainstream feminism that were then in vogue.

The post-slavery period

Black feminism was also very popular during the post-slavery period. Many black females went into action to effect the changes for which black feminism was clamoring. Notable among these women was Frances Ellen Watkins Harper. Although Harper's ideas did not gain much popularity initially, they triggered the black feminist movement. She was the brain behind Reconstruction, gender, and racial equality in the 19th century. The efforts of Harper and other valiant black women helped them break through barriers and make landmark breakthroughs. Some of their achievements included championing the cause of suffrage, giving public lectures, assisting those who were committed to Reconstruction, and other unprecedented landmarks.

Justifying her involvement in the fight for suffrage, Harper noted that black women would derive benefits from suffrage. She cited access to education as one of the benefits while also highlighting the fact that suffrage would give African American women needed protection. She believed the right of black women to vote would give women almost equal power to men and empower black women to have influence and a say in politics, which had always been used as an oppressive tool.

A typical example of what black feminism fought against was the marginalization of women in some civil rights groups. For instance, in the Student Nonviolent Coordinating Committee (SNCC), most of the female members were grossly discriminated against. Many African American women in that civil rights movement were objects of sexism. Some women in this group spoke openly against the way the group treated its female members. In one of the papers they wrote about this discrimination, the women mentioned 11 different events during which female members were considered inferior to men and treated as such. According to these women, all the positions of authority in SNCC were occupied by men while the women were assigned housekeeping and clerical tasks.

The era of Stokey Carmichael saw a significant change in the subjugation of African women in most of these groups, notably in the SNCC. When he was elected chair of the movement, he channeled his efforts towards supporting the ideologies of Black Power. He also ensured that women were treated better. He appointed them to positions of authority, such as project directors. That was a significant change welcomed by the women who were hitherto relegated to the background. However, despite Carmichael's achievements and improvements in the structure of the SNCC, men still occupied its leadership positions.

During the civil rights era, black feminism prospered. It was a time when the evolution of black feminism was defined. The existence of the second-wave movement during the same period of time created the best environment for black feminism to succeed. As racial and gender equality movements were intersectioned, black feminism took its own form and cause. The rise of Black Power with its principles of segregation from whites and the important role of civil rights had a profound impact on the movement and made it a force to be reckoned with among civil rights groups.

Black feminism took its fight into the 21st century. The advancement of science and technology gave black feminism a new dimension as the movement took to the online community. Twitter, Facebook, Tumblr, YouTube, and other social media platforms have been used extensively to promote this movement with a view to uplifting its concept. Many online activists want to leverage the power of new technology to activate dying social justice and gender equality. With these tools, it has now become easier to call out any form of discrimination and immediately challenge it.

The ease of use of social media to fight gender equality has led to the influx of many influential people into the struggle. Many celebrities are now identifying black feminism, racism and sexism and bringing them to the public's attention for redress. Whenever an organization claims to represent black women, black feminists can easily turn to social media to appraise the organization's principles. This has led to a series of condemnations and praise for different organizations in recent years.

For instance, Victoria's Secret held some fashion shows in 2015 and 2016 in which black models were given the opportunity to go on the runway with their natural hair. That single action brought Victoria's Secret several commendations from the international community, especially black movements. That same year, black feminists all over the world applauded the natural hair movement by using these two popular hashtags: #blackgirlmagic and #melanin. The movement had a goal: Black women should feel free to wear their natural hair without being subjected to any form of ridicule.

On the other hand, black feminists used social media to condemn Vogue Italia for one of its 2015 editions. One of the magazine's white models wore afro hair and was given a fake tan to give him a black appearance. The movement considered that action a double standard. They believed that rather than creating a fake blackness, equity demanded that the magazine use a black model. According to the movement, when white people wear afro hair, they are considered edgy or trendy. However, the same hairstyle on black women earns them the derisive term "ghetto." That is obviously the discrimination the movement has been working towards eradicating.

Some notable black feminists in the 21st century include Zendaya, Amandla Stenberg, and Beyonce. These feminists have used their individual talents and skills to champion the cause of black feminism. For instance, Zendaya considers feminism as ensuring fairness and equality for women by empowering them. When Giuliani Rancic, the host of E!, made racist comments against her during the 87th Academy Award, Zendaya took to her Instagram page to address salient issues such as stereotyping, discrimination, body shaming, and ignorance.

Amandla Stenberg considers feminism a very effective tool that can be used to support women's empowerment, dismantle patriarchy, and give discrimination a good fight. She directs her efforts toward intersectionality and ensures that feminism includes a fight for queer women. Cultural appropriation is one of several principles against which Stenberg has fought. She has used her skills as a singer to vehemently fight discrimination. It was no wonder she was named "Feminist of the Year" by the Foundation for Women in 2015. Stenberg was featured in one of Beyonce's music videos, "Formation." The music video encouraged black women to embrace their skin color.

Beyonce has also used her fame and musical skills to good use in supporting the black feminist movement. This has earned her the tag of one of the most influential and famous feminists today. She has used her music as a platform to address the issue of police brutality, feminism, and Black Lives Matter. A couple of her songs have feminist undertones. Some of her music in this category includes "Flawless," "Pretty Hurts," and "Blow." "Blow" focuses on body image, female empowerment, and sexuality. One of Beyonce's studio albums, *Lemonade*, is said to be exclusively produced for black women. She has used her lyrics to address her heritage, culture, marriage, and other issues, including women's empowerment.

Since it was launched some decades ago, the black feminist movement has succeeded in sensitizing the world to the need for black women to receive treatment equal to that of their white counterparts. The contributions of powerful and influential individuals to the cause have been responsible for its success. Without this movement, many black women would still be treated as second-class citizens wherever they live. However, they now have the privilege of enjoying the same benefits their male counterparts and white women enjoy. However, there is another movement that has contributed significantly to the success of this movement. That is the Black Lives Matter movement.

Chapter 15: Black Lives Matter

Black Lives Matter (BLM) originated from the African American community in the United States as an activist movement. The movement demonstrates a high intolerance for racism and violence toward black Africans. To demonstrate its intolerance for such acts, the movement organized and held a series of protests to express its dissatisfaction with the killings of black people by police officers. It also campaigns against racial inequality and profiling in the U.S. This movement achieved some success and made it possible for more African Americans to receive fair treatment in the U.S. justice system.

This movement came into existence in 2013. It began as a protest against the acquittal of an American man who shot to death Trayvon Martin, an African American teen. To campaign against such gross injustice, the hashtag #BlackLivesMatter was created on many social media sites. It gained national recognition in the United States after the death of two black people in 2014. Massive protests were held against the coldblooded murder of those African Americans.

The most notable protests were held in the case of Eric Garner in New York City, and in Ferguson, Missouri. Since the protest that was held in Ferguson, numerous other protests have been held to demand justice for the death of many African Americans at the hands of trigger-happy police or while blacks are in police custody. The founders of #BlackLivesMatter eventually expanded their movement so that it included 30 different groups in just two years, between 2014 and 2016. The movement is decentralized, without a formal hierarchy. All its members also receive equal opportunities to live according to their beliefs without fear of discrimination.

BLM was inspired by earlier movements such as the Black Power movement, civil rights movement, black feminist movement, anti-apartheid movement, and others. These movements fought, in one way or another, for the emancipation of blacks from all forms of discrimination. It's no wonder that some organizations considered the movement a new form of the civil rights movement. However, some members made a distinction between the movement and its predecessors. One of the clear distinctions of Black Lives Matter is members' rejection of middle-class principles such as Democratic Party loyalty, church movement, and respectability politics.

Frederick C. Harris, a political scientist who studied the model of leadership, also noted that BLM is group-centered, unlike other civil rights organizations such as the Rainbow PUSH Coalition and National Action Network. The movement held its first organized national protest in August 2014. Tagged Black Lives Matter Freedom Ride, it involved hundreds of black people who held a peaceful protest in Ferguson, Missouri in response to the assassination of Michael Brown. Although many black groups participated in the protest, Black Lives Matter outperformed all the others.

Hence, the group eventually became the new movement in support of the black community. Since that fateful day in 2014, the group has organized and held thousands of demonstrations and protests. The group has taken it activism to American campuses, as demonstrated by the protests held at the University of Missouri in 2015 and 2016. Black Lives Matter incorporated many ideas outside championing the cause of black freedom. The organization states that the movement has objectives that transcend the extrajudicial killings of African Americans in the United States.

Its principles embrace intersectionality and create room for transgender folks and black queers. Blacks with records and women of different statuses are also protected by the movement. This is interesting considering that all three founders of Black Lives Matter were women with different orientations. Patrisse Cullors and Alicia Garza are queer while Ell Hearns, the third founder, is a transgender woman. The three founders believe their backgrounds make them the right people to found such a great movement.

Both on social media and the official website of the movement, several hashtags such as #BlackQueerLivesMatter, #BlackWomenMatter, #BlackTransLivesMatter, and #BlackGirlsMatter have been used to promote the existence of the movement. They also did much to increase awareness of the movement among blacks around the world, especially African Americans. The all-encompassing nature of the movement has won it admiration at home and abroad. One of the numerous admirers of the movement is Marcia Chatelain, an associate professor of history at the prestigious Georgetown University.

The respected professor praised the movement for giving equal opportunities to queer women, young women, and the like to play a crucial role in the movement. Without any form of discrimination, BLM has helped many black women find a purpose in life and overcome their challenges, including living among people who discriminate against them at will.

The impact of the Internet and social media on the movement

The Internet and social media have created an awareness of this movement. The contribution of black social media users has also played a huge role in affecting the speed at which this movement gained international acceptance and recognition. For instance, the American Dialect Society gave the movement more publicity when it chose #BlackLivesMatter as the official word of the year. A magazine followed in the American Dialect Society's footsteps when it also selected #BlackLivesMatter as among the hashtags that had the most positive impact on the world in 2014.

Memes also played a crucial role in garnering more support for the movement. Leading the list of social media sites that helped promote such memes are Twitter and Facebook. On these platforms, millions of people shared memes that highlighted the objective of the BLM movement. It was believed that this increasing online popularity would have a tremendous impact on the movement's offline acceptance and popularity, too.

One of the most popular phrases related to the movement is "Black Lives Matter." This phrase garnered more than 30 million tweets between the launch of the movement and September 2016. The huge number of tweets is credited with bringing the movement to the international community. By using the hashtag #BlackLivesMatter, activists all over the world have helped show the world the size and strength of their movements. This has also helped them offer other movements with similar goals the moral support and solidarity they need.

BLM guiding principles

Black Lives Matter was formed to fight against the frequent murder of African Americans by the U.S. police and others. To ensure the movement does not lose focus on the reason for its establishment, it is guided by 13 principles. These principles guide all members and help them work with unity of purpose regardless of their backgrounds.

Some of these principles are:

- **Globalism:** Members of the Black Lives Matter movement are expected to see themselves as members of a family regardless of where they come from. This is important considering the fact that members are from different parts of the world and have different backgrounds and upbringings.

- **Restorative Justice:** In contrast to the principle of retributive justice in which offenders are punished in accordance with legal principles, restorative justice allows offenders and victims to achieve a peaceful resolution of their differences through the involvement and assistance of the community. The group claims to be committed to lovingly and collectively working for justice for black people and the world in general. The goal is to ensure that a loving community is intentionally built on love.

- **Collective Value:** The group believes that all black people, regardless of their gender, religious beliefs, sexual identity, disability, economic status, immigration location, or status, should have a collective value that will guide them towards the achievement of their goals.

- **Diversity:** Members are taught to accommodate each other regardless of their differences. They are also taught the act of mutual respect that will boost their ability to accommodate others.

- **Black Women:** The movement is committed to a world where black women can live their lives freely without having to worry about sexism, male-centeredness, and misogyny.

- **Black Villages:** The movement is out to disrupt Western influence on African families. BLM intends to uproot the nuclear family structure recommended by the Western world and revert to the extended family structure in which most Africans grew up. Hence, members should support and treat each other as members of "villages" and extended families. This is to ensure that the responsibility of raising children will be considered a collective responsibility, giving parents and children an opportunity to feel comfortable without undue childhood/parenthood challenges.

- **Intergenerational:** The movement is out to foster an intergenerational network in which ageism is not allowed to serve as an obstacle to progress. Members are taught to consider themselves as one and have equal chances to aspire to any position without the fear of being denied such a privilege based on age.

- **Loving Engagement:** The group seeks to ensure that members embody and practice liberation, justice, and peace in any form of engagement with one another.

- **Queer Affirming:** BLM is governed by the queer affirming principle. The goal of the principle is to help the movement foster a queer-affirming network. In a nutshell, members are encouraged to not consider others as heterosexual unless a member claims to be. This is to encourage members with same-sex relationship tendencies to feel free to express their beliefs without being judged.

- **Empathy:** Empathy is one of the best qualities members are encouraged to develop. Comrades are engaged with the aim of learning about them and identifying their challenges with a view toward proffering solutions to their problems.

- **Unapologetically Black:** BLM members are unapologetic in their quest for freedom. Their affirmation of the continued existence of black people without intimidation should be done without giving up under any condition.

- **Transgender Affirming:** The movement is committed to creating an environment in which cross genders feel at home. The goal is to strip down the wall of discrimination built around transgender people of both sexes.

- **Black Families:** The goal is to make the platform family-friendly and encourage people to participate without discrimination based on gender or age. This is meant to enable children to participate with their parents without any fear of intimidation. The long-standing principle that makes it compulsory for mothers to combine domestic work with secular work will be dismantled so that equality and friendliness can exist within family circles.

The movement has influenced the opinions of many people and has led to landmark achievements. For instance, the Feburary 2015 issue of Essence magazine was devoted to Black Lives Matter. In December of the same year, Time magazine listed BLM as among the contenders for the magazine's Person of the Year.

In the following year, Delrish Moss was sworn in as police chief in Ferguson. He was the first police officer of African descent to hold that post. Moss later acknowledged that the issues he faced, such as improving community relations, diversifying the police force, and other related issues, triggered the need for the BLM movement.

Depictions in the media

Black Lives Matter has received attention in the media. Both in electronic and print media, it has been merited attention that has increased its popularity. For instance:

- It was featured in an episode of the TV series "Law & Order: SVU."

- On March 5, 2015, the TV series "Scandal" depicted the unjust and merciless killing of blacks by white police. In that episode, an unarmed black teenager was shot by white police.

- "Empire," a series on Fox, portrayed the Black Lives Matter movement in its September 28, 2016 episode. It depicted police brutality against blacks when police officers attacked a black man in front of his house despite the fact that he had done nothing wrong.

- In one of its episodes titled "Hope," the ABC sitcom "Black-ish" showed a debate about BLM.

Some notable artists of African origin have also lent their voices to the movement. For instance, in one of her latest videos, "Lemonade," Beyonce featured the mothers of black children who were killed just for the color of their skin. In the video, the three mothers hold the photographs of their slain sons. In another video, "Formation," Beyonce celebrated black culture in the South and featureds policemen who held hands while a black boy danced. In the video, graffiti on a wall reads "Stop shooting us". During demonstrations, some members of BLM have used songs such as "Alright" by Kendrick Lamar.

The movement has also used direct action techniques to drive home the need for people to stand up against injustice against black people. It has used rallies, demonstrations, and protests to indicate their points. In 2015, during the Twin Cities Marathon, the movement staged die-ins, simulating death as a means of protest.

Conclusion

Thank you again for purchasing this book!

I hope this book was able to help you learn more about African American History.

The next step is to share with others what you have learned.

Finally, if you enjoyed this book, then I'd like to ask you for a favor, would you be kind enough to leave a positive review for this book on Amazon? It would be greatly appreciated!

Preview of "History of China" by Adam Brown

Chapter 1: Ancient Chinese Dynasties

Overview of Dynasties

A dynasty, in Chinese literature, refers to a series of rulers from the same family and historical periods named after the family that dominated the country at the time. Some dynasties lasted for many centuries while others were in power for only a few years. The earliest dynasty began with the first ruler in 2200 BC and ended in 1912 with the last Emperor of China. From 1912 to 1949, the country that was previously Imperial China became the Republic of China. Thus, more than 4000 years of dynasties came to an end when the last emperor was forced to leave his seat. From 1949 onwards, the country became known as the People's Republic of China, which continues today.

1: Xia Dynasty (2200 – 1600 BC)

Around 2200 BC, the occupants of what is now Northern China near the Yellow River came under the rule of the Xia Dynasty. There is little evidence for this dynasty's existence apart from some records that were compiled much later by reliable historians. It is theorized that the people began to use bronze during this time due to some evidence suggesting that bronze casting occurred at Erlitou during the Xia Dynasty.

Legend states that it was Yu the Great (2200-2100 BC) who began the dynasty. He was a hard worker among the early settlers who helped to ensure the safety of his people. It is documented that the Yellow River constantly flooded the land

and caused great difficulty among the people. Crops would be ruined, homes would flood and the people would complain about the hardship that they were in. Yu the Great is known for building dams that ultimately helped to stop flooding in his community and he became well-known for his nobility, leading to the people choosing him as their ruler. Thus, the very first dynasty was founded. The Xia Dynasty had 17 kings and continued until 1600 BC when the Shang Dynasty came into power.

2: Shang Dynasty (1600 – 1046 BC)

Jie of the Xia Dynasty had begun to oppress the people through taxation and unjust laws that were enacted only to benefit the nobility. The people who suffered the most were peasants, who worked long hours and earned meager wages, and occupied the lower strata of society. Because of the hardship many suffered at the hands of the Xia rule at this time, a rebellion began. People threw their support behind Chen Tang, who convinced them they needed a new king. The revolt spread until Jie, the last Xia emperor, was overthrown by a final battle known as the Battle of Mingtiao. Most of Jie's army either deserted the plain of battle or surrendered to the stronger force of Chen Tang. Thus around 1600 BC, the Shang Dynasty came to power.

Western scholars previously used to debate the existence of the Shang Dynasty because much of the knowledge came only from Ancient Chinese literature. However during the 1920s, archaeological excavations unearthed considerable evidence for its existence. Scholars believe that the Shang Dynasty achieved much more progress than the Xia dynasty but this may be due to the minimal historical data about the Xia Dynasty. Nonetheless, major cities and urban hubs including

Anyang and Zhengzhou were established during the Shang Dynasty. At its height, the Shang State only controlled a relatively small area of northern China but their rule became a model for other rival States including the Zhou State.

Manufacturing of bronze is known to have continued during this time period. Brass was made from the abundant suppliers of copper, tin and lead that were dug by the Chinese. The miners provided these metals to blacksmiths, who smelted them into bronze. Most bronze was used for ornaments and for ritual objects while only a small amount was used for weaponry and agriculture.

The Shang organized society in a form of feudalism in which relatives of the king and other nobles were granted land in return for their service and loyalty. This resulted in the kings having a great deal of power, and like the kings before thim, were more at risk of abusing that power. The last Shang king was accused of drunkenness, incest, cannibalism, sadism, and was considered evil. The virtues that had once led to the elevation of the Shang were decimated as a result. Once again, there was an uprising against the tyrant king. Sensing vulnerability, Wu Wang from the east attacked the Shang empire and came to power after winning the Battle of Muye. The defeat of the last Shang king (who ironically had been named King Zhou at his own coronation) in 1046BC effectively began the Zhou Dynasty.

3: The Zhou Dynasty (1046 – 256 BC)

Wu Wang became the first king of the Zhou Dynasty after the Shang fell from power. The dynasty lasted until 256 BC, making it the longest to rule for nearly 800 years. The kings had learned from their predecessors and did not make many of the same mistakes. Wu Wang is known to have established the concept of the "Mandate of Heaven". The people believed that the king was appointed by the divine and only the appointed individual had the right to rule in China. The ancient Egyptian pharoahs had a similar concept in which it was believed the pharoah was the closest to the gods and appointed by the divine.

For Wu Wang, this served two purposes. First, this solidified his claim on the throne as legitimate and unquestionable. He was then not a conquering king but a destined king. Secondly, the mandate quenched any possible dissent with the argument that as a king from the divine, he was the only person fit to rule. This made it more difficult to question the king's ability as ruler, which had led to the previous dynasty's demise. After all, Wang had been sent as the solution to the Shang Emperor, was disgraced by his lack of virtue. The Zhou Dynasty was the third and the last of three Pre-Imperial dynasties.

In the course of the Zhou Dynasty, there were 39 kings who followed one another mostly through father to son succession. Initially, the Zhou Dynasty began well by building a successful defense of the country against the barbarians in the West. However as the centuries passed, the country became disunited and there was a great deal of internal strife. Despite this, there were major advancements in the organization of society, technology, construction, trade and agriculture. Some very important features of Chinese thought and philosophy also came to the forefront during this time, the most notable of which are Confucianism and Tao religion.

In the three pre-Imperial dynasties the ruler was viewed as a king who was both a leader and a warrior. Because he was an intermediary to the divine who resided in heaven, the king would perform rituals with the help of his ministers to speak with his ancestors and the divine. Relics called *Oracle bones* were heated up and the cracks that formed on these bones were interpreted as answers to the questions they asked about the future. Questions inscribed on these bones are among the earliest examples of writing that we have today.

4: The Qin Dynasty (221 – 207 BC)

The Qin Dynasty came to power when Qin Shi Huang defeated the last Zhou king at the Battle of Changping, beginning the First Imperial Dynasty. Shi Huang was the first Emperor of China, because he was the first to successfully control the seven states under his rule. The philosophy of Confucianism was abandoned and replaced with Legalism, which led to a great strengthening and centralization of the state. Shi Huang was a ruthless man who suffered from constant paranoia that others would invade his empire. It was during his reign that the Great Wall of China began construction to protect the outskirts of the empire.

His tomb was surrounded by the statues of the famous Terracotta Army who were meant to fight for the Emperor in the afterlife. Shi Huang had been an unpopular ruler due to his ruthlessness and when he died, the Qin dynasty came to an end. The first emperor is thought to have consumed an elixir that was supposed to grant him eternal life. Instead, it is believed, that elixir is what killed him, and today, scholars believe that he died from mercury poisoning. Nonetheless, through his unification of the seven states, he initiated a chain of rulers that would become known as the Emperors of China.

5: The Han Dynasty (206 BC – 220 AD)

After the death of Qin Shi Huang, the Han Dynasty came to power when the first ruler named himself Emperor Gaozu. Gaozu had come from the lower classes in society and was initially very stubborn in taking advice from his ministers despite their knowledge of the state and how to rule. It is believed he realized the error of his ways when he heard some words of wisdom from his beautiful chamberlain, named Lu Jia, who eventually bore Gaozu a son. The emperor took careful notice of the warning and began to place greater faith in the abilities of his ministers. The Han Dynasty is viewed to be a good dynasty that ruled over a peaceful, wealthy and vast empire. Gaozu gave land and possessions to his relatives and supporters so he could build a strong group of allies. The feudal system was re-established like it had been present during the Zhou era but it slowly diminished as new Han rulers replaced each other over time.

Many power struggles occurred within the families of the emperors because they fathered sons through a number of women. During Gaozu's final years, a bitter fight took place between Lu Jia who had given birth to the Gaozu's favourite son, and the Emperor's favorite, Qi, who had hopes that the succession would go to her own child. Qi's son was the Emperor's preferred heir but when he died in 195 BC, the succession went to Lu Jia's son instead. After the Emperor died, when Lu Jia became the Empress dowager, she began to rule China as regent. When her son died she installed another boy as emperor to maintain her power. However, when the boy grew up, a power struggle began between him and Lu Jia; feeling threatened, she had him replaced as well. She is known to have granted power to her relatives by removing noble families through bloody purges and by giving their estates to her own relatives. Lu Jia remained in power until her death in 180 BC. In the power struggle that followed her death, the family of the Empress dowager was annihilated.

The Han Dynasty went through a time of consolidation, with China expanding southwards and venturing into Vietnam and Korea. The severities of the Qin legal code were steadily reduced so as to make the new status quo popular among the people. The Han Dynasty lasted for over 400 years and were interrupted only once by the brief rebellion and coup of Wang Mang. The dynasty witnessed long periods of prosperity and was notable for advances in the manufacturing of iron, hydraulics and paper. Its influence was so great that the Chinese finally began to see a unified empire as something normal after being divided for hundreds of years. This normalization of the unification benefited the Hans, as the people referred to themselves as the 'Sons of Han' and regarded the Han Empire as a model for the future.

This would change with the fall of the Han Dynasty. The deterioration of the Han Empire can be compared to the decline of the Roman Empire, both of which experienced a long period of power struggles upon their deterioration. After the fall of the Han, there were a total of six dynasties that fought for power during this period in Chinese history, and divided the land once more.

6: The Six Dynasties (220 AD – 589 AD)

The Six Dynasties period of China began from the end of the Han dynasty in 220 A.D. and continued until the rise of the Sui Dynasty in 589 A.D. The dynasties were as follows:

Wu (222-280 AD),

Dong Jin (317 – 420 AD),
Liu-Song (420 - 479 AD),
Nin Qi (479 - 502 AD),
Nan Liang (502-557 AD),
Nan Chen (557-589 AD).

These periods of short rule were marked by struggles between landowners and peasants, between the military and the large number of non-ethnic Chinese who had settled in the North, and between the officials and local rulers. China was divided into what is known as the Three Kingdoms: Wei in the North, Shu in the Southwest and Wu in the South. While the 6 dynasties fought, there was never one Emperor to rule a united China. During the period 317-420, Dong Jin supposedly ruled over a part of China called the 16 Kingdoms, but they were not really under his control. The Chinese have long been fascinated by the personalities, conflicts, and literary works that exist from this period.

The 6 dynasties brought about an age of appalling violence and bloodshed, which is not very different from the last 400 years of European history. However, this period also witnessed a flowering of Chinese literature and some radical cultural changes. The most significant change came with the spread of Buddhism. The religion became an integral part of the Chinese way of life in which Confucianism, Taoism and Buddhist values complemented each other, beginning to construct the rich tapestry that is Chinese ideology and culture today.

7: The Sui Dynasty (581 – 618 AD)

The Sui dynasty began in 581 AD and lasted for 37 years with only 2 emperors. A struggle occurred in Northern Zhou when the Duke of Sui replaced Yuwen Pin as the local ruler. The Duke of Sui is known to have had a mixed ethnicity and he took the name Sui Wengdin when he became Emperor. Wengdin was a brutal man but he reunited China through highly planned and brilliant military campaigns. During his rule, the Buddhist religion flourished because nearly 4000 temples and pagodas were built with his approval. Clauses that called for prohibitions against both Buddhism and Taoism were also abolished during his reign.

Sui Wengdin was succeeded by his youngest son Sui Yangdin who was notorious for his cruelty and ruthlessness. This ascension to power came about by plotting against his older brother, killing his father, and raping a number of his father's wives. He exploited slaves to build canals and to advance the building projects in China. Unlike his father, however, Sui Yangdin was not a brilliant military strategist, which had been essential for Sui Wengdin to come to power. One of the main things that contributed to the downfall of the dynasty under Sui Yangdin's rule was a series of disastrous military campaigns against the Koreans. This eventually led to Sui Yangdin fleeing after a military defeat, and the fall of the Sui dynasty.

8: The Tang Dynasty (618 – 907 AD)

The first ruler of this Dynasty was a man called Li Yuan who replaced Sui Yangdin, declaring himself emperor and crowning himself a Tang Gaozu. His son, Tang Taizong became the second Tang ruler and is known to have been a brilliant emperor because he was wise enough to take constructive criticism and advice from his ministers. His most trusted advisor, Wei Zhang, helped him to become a noble ruler to the point that he was eventually seen as a saint after his death. Tang Gaozong, the third Tang ruler, is known to have married the famous Empress Wu. When he passed away, she became the only female ruler in Chinese history.

Empress Wu was a capable ruler despite being recorded in a most unfavorable way by the historians of China. Confucianism regarded women as second class citizens and did not allow them to lead the Empire. Empress Wu challenged this view and despite the dissent and sexism, led the country in a more peaceful direction. The century between 650 and 750 AD was a wondrous period of time for the Chinese. The Chinese empire was economically restored through trade with India, Persia, Vietnam, Korea and Japan.

The apex of the Tang period occurred during the reign of Tang Xuanzong, who was in power from 712 to 756 AD. Buddhism continued to flourish in the Tang period and its influence grew among the people. During the Tang Dynasty, the capital city alternated between Chang'an and Luo Yang. The Tang Dynasty continued to push the idea that safeguarding of the borders of the empire was a task best suited to non-Han people. This policy ultimately paved the way for the disasters that came soon afterwards.

At this time, a man named An Lushan of non-Chinese pedigree had made his way into Imperial favor. He had an affair with one of the Emperor's mistresses named Yang Guifei, who was known to be very beautiful. When the Emperor discovered the affair, An Lushan was forced to flee the capital. Because An Lushan felt he had lost honor by fleeing, he raised an army and sacked the capital of Chang'an. This time, the Emperor fled with his mistress Yang Guifei and his chief Minister Yang Guozhong. Both of the Yangs were killed but the Emperor escaped during the flight. An Lushan was not able to take full control and so the Tang Emperor eventually abdicated in favor of his son Tang Suzong. The Tangs regained their capital Chang'an and the core of the empire but their high tide had passed. In the late ninth century, Huang Chao led a campaign against the Tangs and captured the capital of Chang'an, this time managing to keep it. The Tang Dynasty finally came to an end and was followed by a short period of quick succession called the Five Dynasties period.

9: The Five Dynasties (907 – 960 AD)

This was a very short period in the long history of China that covered the years between 907 and 960 A.D. It was a time of much disorder during which China splintered into 10 kingdoms with a total of 40 different rulers. It seems historians remember this era only for the complete political disaster that occurred over the years. However, two significant inventions were made that revolutionized society during this time, and we continue to use them today.

Firstly, a printing press with a movable typing board was invented to write accounts of Chinese ancestors. The bureaucrat Feng Dao is known to have compiled various works using this new technology at the time. He created many biographies in his loyal service to the Five Dynasties but was seen negatively by other biographers. Secondly, the Chinese came up with the idea of using paper money as the main form of currency. It was easy to produce and did not weigh as much as coins that other people in the world were using at the time. As a result, there was a surge in trade and commerce in some of the kingdoms. Because of political strife, the capital was shifted back and forth between Luo Yang and Kaifeng by the rulers. In any case, Chang'an was abandoned and never used again because it had become a city of ruins.

10: The Song Dynasty (960 – 1297 AD)

The first Song emperor was Song Taizu who came to power after the Empire had experienced long periods of political instability. He ruled with the assistance of his generals to control the people until he died in 976 AD. During the Song Dynasty, there was a great flowering of arts in China and an expansion of Confucian philosophy among the working class. The anti-martial ethos of Confucianism came to dominate China and the military allowed much of the power to be distributed among the people so they did not have to intervene in state affairs.

During the reign of the first two emperors, the empire was expanded to push the borders further out again. Initially, the Song Dynasty was centered at Kaifeng in the north and called the Northern Song Dynasty. The center of the empire was transferred to Lin'an in South China after a defeat against the Jin. In 1235, the Song Empire made a terrible mistake by attacking the Mongols who had at that point established themselves as the greatest military power in the world. The Mongols fought back and brought the Song Dynasty to an end.

11: The Yuan Dynasty (1271 – 1368 AD)

Kublai Khan became the ruler of China in 1271 AD and the Emperor in 1279 AD. His name as Emperor was Shizu of Yuan and he founded the first and only non-Chinese dynasty known as the Yuan Dynasty. He moved the capital of China to Beijing, which was not too far from Mongolia. He did this to ensure that his troops did not become "softened" by being stationed in China for so long, as China was seen as militarily "inferior" due to their defeat. The Chinese were forced to pay an extra tax to the Mongols who needed to finance their occupation and expenses. Because of the foreign invasion with no attempt to assimilate with or even appease the Chinese people, Mongol rule was not very popular in China and the people rose up to regain control of their country, achieving independence in 1368.

12: The Ming Dynasty (1368 -1644 AD)

In 1368, Ming Hongwu became the first Chinese Emperor after the Yuan Dynasty was removed from power. He was the first emperor of the Ming Dynasty, which lasted from 1368 to 1644 AD. Ming Hongwu was a bloodthirsty man who did not like the Mandarins and killed thousands of them without any just reason, leading to a decline in popularity and trust. Ming Hongwu's son, Ming Yongle, became the third Ming emperor after he proved himself to be a brilliant soldier. He was obsessed with exploration and expansion of the empire and sent out thousands of soldiers to places near the Indian Ocean, Australia and even to America. Unfortunately, all sea-based expeditions ceased after Yongle died in 1424.

In 1517, the Portuguese arrived and caused significant change, although the Mings did not realize what was happening until it was too late. The Europeans claimed they were visiting only to trade with the Chinese. Initially there was no threat but the responsibilities of the Emperors declined slowly as the Europeans began to influence them. In 1644, the last Ming Emperor hung himself on a hill over Beijing because a rebel leader had successfully seized the city.

13: The Qing Dynasty (1644 – 1912)

The Qing Dynasty was the last imperial dynasty of China and consisted of foreign rulers that were Manchus in origin. Unlike the Mongols, they had adopted Chinese customs and were mostly regarded as Chinese, leading to a relatively more stable rule. The empire expanded its borders to include the various territories that China controls today. In 1689, the Qings defeated the Russians in the siege of Albazin and took control of the area, but diminished in power when the British arrived. The British sold large amounts of opium to the Chinese and essentially liquidated their economy. Then, they fought a war with them that the Chinese had no chance of winning.

As a consequence, the British were able to establish a strong foothold in China. Empress Cixi came to power and allied herself with some rebels called the Boxers. They declared war on the foreigners but were not successful. In addition, the Chinese had also been invaded by the Japanese in a war prior to fighting the British so they were left severely weakened. The empress died in 1908 and the Qing Dynasty ended in 1911. Thus, the famous dynasties of China that had ruled for over 4000 years finally came to an end.

Chapter 2: Communism, Capitalism and Its Role in Shaping China & East Asia

China

A revolution took place in southern China during October 1911 that led to the end of the Qing dynasty. It was then that the Republic of China was formed with the first leader being Sun Yat Sen. As is always the case in revolutions, there was utter chaos from 1916 to 1925 because different warlords were ruling separate regions. There was a deep resentment among the people because China had been attacked and humiliated by foreign powers repeatedly in the 19th century, and these foreign nations still had some power in Shanghai and other areas of China. Sun Yat Sen appealed to Britain and America for recognition of his democratic regime at Canton. He asked for assistance to overthrow the treacherous warlords that had gained power but his appeal was rejected. The warlords were weak and corrupt and did not care for China's interests. They loved the loopholes in the foreign policy that they could use for their own benefit when things went awry. As such, they were able to invest their ill-gotten gains safely under the protection of foreign policy.

The inspiration for the Chinese Revolution came from democracy but it was not recognized by the West. As a consequence, the Chinese revolutionaries themselves rejected it. They turned to communism because of Russia's promise for help, encouragement and equal treatment. In 1921, Sun Yat Sen met the Russian envoy Joffe in Shanghai. After much discussion they concluded that communism was not the best system for China. Nonetheless, Sun Yat Sen accepted Russian aid with the new Chinese Communist Party on behalf of the Kuomintang, or the Nationalist Party.

The Kuomintang Party became just like the Russian Communist Party. It had political commissions, mass propaganda outlets and organizations to ensure strict discipline. It did not work for a democratic republic but for a party dictatorship, which ran the country for several years until the people were able to govern themselves. The Chinese Communist party was founded in 1921 by a group of people including Mao Zedong and Choi Enlai. Mao Zedong was a library assistant in Chien's University and Choi Enlai was studying in Paris. Mao came from the middle peasant or yeoman class of people that were classified as land owners. Thus, his father was a farmer and was able to provide an education for his son. As for Chou, he came from a wealthy Mandarin background so there was no financial issue when he decided to study abroad.

None of these early foundation members and later leaders had seen communism in Russia nor understood the Russian language. This had significant ramifications later on as the decades passed and the country became unstable. After the death of Yat Sen in 1925, the Kuomintang prepared an expedition from their base in Canton to conquer the north and to remove the warlords from power. The Kuomintang wanted genuine reform and put together a loyal army of supporters, but foreign powers were certain that the Kuomintang would never defeat the more martial northerners. The expedition began under the leadership of Chiang Kai-shek in early 1926. Chiang Kai-shek had previously been sent for special training in Moscow by Sun Yat Sen so he was readily able to take command of the new military training college at Whampoa. This college produced the best-known generals of the

Kuomintang and also the future leading generals of the communist army. The expedition turned out to be a victory as the northern warlords were overcome one by one. The Kuomintang strategy was simple: use the warlords' own people against them. As the southern soldiers closed in on Shanghai, a social revolution began to appear. The communist organizers spread through the rural areas, inciting the peasants against their landlords while others created tension among the poor workers of Shanghai.

When news reached the Shanghai workers about the southern army, they seized parts of the city from the warlords under the communist leadership of Chou En-Lai. When the Nationalist armies arrived from the south, both the workers and the warlords' men confronted the forces of the revolution.

Chiang Kai-shek had known for a long time that his alliance with the communist revolution could not last forever. He was in danger of losing his position of leadership because the Nationalist government was now based in Wu Han, because the city was very left-wing and under the influence of Russian advisors. These advisors insisted that the communists should help the Kuomintang carry out the revolution. Instead, Chiang Kai-shek struck and executed those communist leaders that he could catch. However, Chou Enlai managed to escape to the north and Chiang Kai-shek was not able to catch him.

Chiang Kai-shek separated from the Wu Han government to set up his own right-wing Nationalist government based in Nanking. This break from the Communist Party caused the beginning of the Chinese revolution, of which the communists emerged as the victors in 1949. At the same time, the Japanese, taking advantage of the turmoil, were conquering large areas of China. In a drastic move, Chiang Kai-shek ignored the Japanese and devoted his time and energy to destroy the communists through his campaigns. The communists could not be defeated, but Chiang Kai-shek persisted in his attacks for ten years.

Meanwhile, Mao and his colleagues established a new kind of communist regime. Its main interests included land reform, the use of guerilla tactics in warfare and the incitement of peasants for political aim. This was absolute heresy according to Russian and conventional Marxist teachings, and Mao was expelled from the Central Political Committee for creating this regime. Some say he was purged from the party but there is no clear evidence to indicate such a thing. For years Mao's communists were cut off from the rest of the world, so they were not able to obtain orders from Moscow.

First, Mao's communists exploited the peasants through their hunger for land. They encouraged peasants to kill landlords publicly in a cruel manner. Officials of the Kuomintang were executed and non-supporters received harsh treatment for speaking up. To avoid Chiang Kai-shek, the communists mimicked the long march of Huang Chao from the ninth century and walked to Yenan. They set up their base in the caves with supplies, medication and ammunition. It was from there that they launched the campaigns that led them to eventually become rulers of China. The Kuomintang Party could have prevented this but it feared the Ancient Chinese social system. It tried to alter the direction of the revolution and to bring stability to the society while still clinging on to the past. Ultimately, the Kuomintang failed because of selfishness, greed and nepotism.

By 1936, the communists had completed their Long March and established themselves as a military power in China. In

December 1936, Chiang Kai-shek planned one more 'extermination drive' against the communists in Xi'an. The army consisted of local Shensi forces and the north-eastern fighters that were loyal to Chiang. However, the threat of the Japanese was growing, and before he could carry out the attack, Chiang Kai-shek was captured and forced to sign an agreement with the communists to fight the Japanese. The agreement lasted only up until the Japanese were defeated and driven out of China. At the end of the war, Chiang Kai-shek requested the U.S. Air Force to transport his troops to the areas occupied by the communists. The idea was to ensure that the Japanese surrendered to the Kuomintang rather than to the communists, giving Kuomintang more leverage and public respect. In addition, the Japanese were ordered to hold all ground against the communists and to surrender only to the Kuomintang forces. So when the American forces flew in with soldiers to where the Japanese were holding territory, the communists were outraged. This was absolutely unacceptable for them and they developed a hatred for America as a result of this interference.

The Russians betrayed the communists in a different way. The Russians had occupied Manchuria since the end of the Second World War and could have handed this region over to the Chinese communists. Instead, they gave over the cities to the Kuomintang and stole all resources from the factories so the communists were forced to gather on the countryside. Despite this betrayal, the Communists won the civil war that raged until 1949. When the war was over, Mao ascended the Gates of Heavenly Peace and proclaimed, "This country will never again be insulted by foreigners. We have taken a stand against them". After the civil war, there was a period of calm and reformations were made to protect the people.

In October 1950, China became involved in the Korean War and 3 million Chinese soldiers were sent to fight in the war. About 200,000 died, including Mao's oldest son Mao Anying. This was also around the time where the world's superpowers were amassing weapons of mass destruction, and Mao himself was very keen to obtain an atomic bomb during this time, but he did not have the resources or funds to build it. He had hoped he would be able to get them from Russia, whose leader at the time was Stalin.

However, In 1956, Krushchev became the new leader of Russia, denouncing Stalin as a murderer. Mao wasn't able to form the same relationship with Krushchev that he'd had with Stalin. as a result, he wasn't able to get the atomic weapons he had been hoping for.

The years after the Korean War marked a time of great strife and inner conflict in China, as well as an increase in animosity between China and Russia. After the Korean War, Mao began requisitioning grain from the peasants and caused great hardship among the people who occupied lower stratas of society. The situation became worse when the peasants were forced to live in collective farms in 1955. At the same time, he nationalized all industry and commerce. In 1957 Mao said, "Let 100 flowers bloom," the iconic statement which meant he would allowing people to speak their minds. While this seemed liberating and a moment of hope for the people, they were punished when they spoke up. They were arrested, humiliated and tortured for views that were contrary to Mao's policies. In 1958, he launched the Great Leap Forward to manufacture significant materials to be used in future wars. This ended in disaster, as it caused millions of people to die from starvation. In 1959, Mao ordered the invasion of Tibet because he believed the region to have always been a part of

China. In 1960, the animosity between Khrushchev and Mao became public after Mao declared that he was not afraid of a nuclear war provided that the communists emerged as the victors. The Russians strongly disagreed with this statement and withdrew their advisors from China.

In 1962, Mao began a brief and indecisive war with India which only led to more lives being lost and dissent among his people. However, he pressed on in his effort to expand military strength, and in 1964, the Chinese finally tested their first nuclear weapon at Lop Nor, in a remote part of China. The radiation released as a result is thought to have killed hundreds of thousands of people. Throughout his reign, Mao was an iconoclast who destroyed many of the architectural and artistic treasures of the Chinese past. He also deprived the people of entertainment because he did not feel it aligned well with communist principles. People were force-fed propaganda and Mao had a personality that was very similar to that which exists in North Korea today. In 1966, the Cultural Revolution began and millions of people were killed. In 1969, there was a rumor that suggested Russia and America were planning to attack the Chinese nuclear facilities. America refused to acknowledge such a plot when asked, and this led to extraordinary events in the next four decades.

1972 brought a rapprochement between the USA and China. President Richard Nixon held meetings with Mao and began a process of negotiation and tense allyship that persists to this day. Mao died in 1976 from Lou Gehrig's disease, and it is stated that he suffered from paranoia. Deng Xiaoping came to power in 1978 and in an effort to distance himself from the previous leader, initiated great changes in policy. He freed many innocent people who had been persecuted and imprisoned during Mao's reign. However, Deng Xaioping is not free from controversy. He is most popularly known for initiating the one-child policy as a form of population control, and beginning trade with all countries. As a result, China went through a lot of reforms such that an impoverished country previously imprisoned with Stalinist communism was completely changed.

China's new rulers embraced capitalism in all ways except calling referring to it as *capitalism* because of the conflict with the USA. They did not want to be viewed as adopting the same principles as America. As a result, the Communist Party remains communist by name only and its main function is to control the population and manage dissent within the people. With the USA repudiating its policies against global warming and free trade, China has an opportunity to showcase its way of doing things to the entire world. In January 2017, the leader of China attended a meeting of the world's best and most powerful economic leaders and declared Chinese support for free trade. China has already created the best solar industry in the world. If it can find ways to successfully limit global warming, it may yet dominate the world in almost all areas. This form of foresight and investment in environmentally friendly and economically beneficial reform is what helps China to remain a strong international presence and leader today.

East Asia, Asia, and the Pacific

In the 15th century, Vasco da Gama of Portugal rounded the Cape of Good Hope and reached Asia. This began what would become centuries of interaction between Europe and the countries of the Asian continent. Initially, the European countries only came with a declared intention to trade, but later they conquered many of these countries and set up colonies. The colonization of Asia by the Europeans was largely complete by the end of the 19th century.

During the 19th century, Japan had become a major industrial power in the North Pacific. It built a huge fleet and defeated the Russians in a war that occurred at the beginning of the 20th century. The Japanese attacked and colonized Korea in 1910 to expand the borders of their empire. After the First World War, they set their sights on China.

In 1940, Japan took the opportunity to seize Vietnam while the European powers fought amongst themselves in World War Two. The Japanese attacked America and Britain in 1941 and became the first to attack United States soil. They faced the American forces in a three and a half year war in which there were millions of casualties. America definitively ended the battle by dropping atomic bombs on Hiroshima and Nagasaki, devastating the country and millions of people.

By the end of the Second World War, all of Asia and much of Europe began the long journey to recovery. For Asia, this journey became even longer. The European powers were all exhausted politically and economically and so they no longer had the resources to run the colonies they had set up in Asia. The first of the European countries to realize this was Britain, and after increased dissent and rebellion throughout the region, it lost India and Pakistan to become independent countries in 1947. There were other British colonies in Asia, but they had been saved from the horrors that occurred in the colonies of other European countries. Holland controlled what was then called the Dutch East Indies but was defeated by the Nazi onslaught in early 1940. At the end of the war, it tried to reassert its authority but the people living in the region gained independence and changed the country's name to Indonesia.

Indonesia

Indonesia gained its independence in 1949 when Sukarno became the first president. The government is democracy but it nearly became a communist government in 1965. There was a mini-revolution after which Suharto became the new leader. Mao encouraged the communists in Indonesia to have a revolution, but it failed and millions died. Indonesia is the largest Muslim majority country in the world and the 5th largest producer of coal. The country remains a democracy and has a population of about 260 million people. There are nearly three million Chinese people living in Indonesia today.

Indochina

Since the early 19th century, France had been in control of Indochina. This region consists of a group of countries including Cambodia, Laos, and Vietnam. After the Second World War, the French tried to reassert their colonial control, but like many European countries, failed. Their attempts came to an end in 1954 with the battle of Den Bien Phu when Ho Chi Minh led the Vietnamese rebels to victory against the French army. As a consequence, France left Indochina and those countries became independent. Unfortunately, in the turmoil that followed, Vietnam was divided into two parts. North Vietnam became a communist country led by Ho Chi Minh and the rebels. South Vietnam was a very unstable country like China had been before the Communists took over. It was the desire of Ho Chi Minh to unite both parts of Vietnam into one country but he was not able to accomplish his goals, because the United States interfered during the Vietnam War.

The United States led a coalition of nations that successfully prevented the communists from taking over the entire Korean peninsula in the 1950s. The US was also anxious to keep communists out of South Vietnam because it had trade vessels that travelled near the area. From 1954 to 1972, the US unsuccessfully waged a war with the help of a number of allies against the South Vietnamese rebels known as the Vietcong. The Allies were trying their best to keep the communists from coming to power in North Vietnam. During this war, they dropped three times the capacity of bombs that were dropped by all of the warring countries combined during World War II. The Americans left Indochina in 1975 after realizing that they needed to focus more on the affairs of their home country.

Initially, Cambodia, Laos and a reunited Vietnam became communist countries. Vietnam is similar to China in that it retained its Communist Party throughout its government. All of the countries in South East Asia are very rich in resources and they use them to maintain their economies. Although trade is conducted with various countries, the most significant trade partner is China. It seems that China will eventually have the most influence in South East Asia because of its growing economy and increasing number of exports.

India

India is a huge Asian country with strong links to both China and the rest of Asia. It is not an East Asian country but it has a lot of history with China, as both were once large empires that were then invaded by the British. India was never a communist country, but it had a very socialist economy until the late 20th century. Although it has not transformed itself as much as China, it is certainly making great progress and has become a major world power. India has a huge population and vast resources that it uses to trade with the West. India fought a brief war with China in 1962 because of disputes that occurred on the border. There have been a few problems since then but overall, like their dealings in the past, India and China maintain close ties until today.

www.ingramcontent.com/pod-product-compliance
Lightning Source LLC
Chambersburg PA
CBHW071240070526
44583CB00017B/2261